たくや式

どんどん読める

中学英語

長文 ④

藤井拓哉

中2 比較

朝日学生新聞社

はじめに

　本書は、中学英語の長文読解を、学年別にステップアップしながら身につけようというコンセプトでつくりました。文法の詳しい解説は、『たくや式中学英語ノート』（朝日学生新聞社）全10巻で紹介しましたので、ここでは割愛しています。

　この本では、練習問題を解きながら英語の読解テクニックを学ぶだけでなく、

① 英語の長文（会話・メール・手紙など）の特徴
② 英語での意見の述べ方
③ 日本語にはない、英語ならではの表現

といった『たくや式中学英語ノート』であまり練習できなかった内容を身につけてもらうのが大きな目的です。また、ただ問題を解くだけでなく、

長文全ての和訳と「なぜそのような訳になるのか？」といった
細かい文法の説明もできるように練習する

ことも行います。その理由は「基礎中の基礎である中学英語は、しっかり理解しておかないと難度が高くなった時に必ずつまずくから」です。英語が得意という方に「どうやって英語を学びましたか？」とたずねると「教科書を丸暗記した」という答えがよく返ってきますが、これは（記憶力が、ものすごくいい方は別として）「教科書に登場する全ての文を、なぜそうなるのか、しっかり説明できるぐらい理解できている」と言っているのと同じことだと思います。

長文とはお手本となる文を集めたようなもの。お手本となる文章が「なぜそうなるのか」「なぜこの表現がここで使われるのか」を、説明できるようになることを私は読者のみなさんに求めています。

　また読者のみなさんには長文を通じて「英語ならではの表現」や「英語での考え方」といった「英語の世界観」も理解してもらいたいと思っています。「英語のアウトプット（スピーキング・ライティング）を向上させたければ、インプット（リーディング・リスニング）をしっかり練習しなさい」と主張する英語教員もたくさんいますが、これは「お手本となる文にたくさん触れ、自分のものにし、しっかり使いこなせるようにする」という意見です。実際、私も本やニュースなどで登場したフレーズを真似して使うことがよくあります。

　「なるほど、ネイティブはこうやって使うんだ」「こんな言い回しがあるのか」「こういう時は、この前置詞か」などインプットから学べるものは、非常に多いです。そのため、読者のみなさんにも日本語とはちがう英語の世界も、この本を通じて学んでもらいたいと考えています。

　本書はその回までに学んだ文法や単語を中心に英文を作成していますので、多少ぎこちない表現も登場しますが、シリーズを通じて、段階を追って英文読解ができる内容となっています。基礎的な読解力を身につけたいという方だけでなく、アウトプットを含めた全体的な英語力の向上を目指す方にも、ご利用いただけたら幸いです。

藤井拓哉

この本の特長

特長1　学年別にステップアップする単語・文法を使った長文

　本書は、中学で習う英語長文を、学年別に学びます。単語や文法もその学年で学ぶ内容を使ったオリジナルの長文を掲載し、どの学年の方でも無理なく長文を読めるようになっています。

特長2　すべての問題をネットビデオ講義で解説！

　すべての問題を、著者の藤井拓哉先生が解説したビデオ講義をインターネットを通じて見ることができます。発音をチェックしたり、音読の練習に役立てたりしてください。ビデオ講義の詳細は7ページをご覧ください。

特長3　豊富な問題と全文和訳で、英語長文を完全理解！

　1つの長文につき、約10問の問題が設定されています。高校入試やテストでよく出題される選択問題や穴埋め問題に加えて、英語の文法を正しく理解しているかを確認できる「たくや式」ならではの問題も収録されています。また、長文の全文和訳に挑戦することで、単語や文法の抜けに気づくことができ、完全な理解に近づけます。

この本の使い方

Step1

長文を読んで、問題にチャレンジ　＊印のついている単語・語句には、本文の後に説明があります。

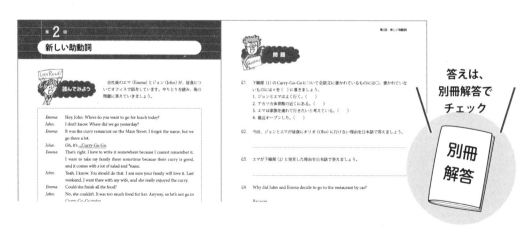

Step2

「ここがポイント」で確認事項
をチェック

Step3

全文和訳にチャレンジ

和訳例は、
別冊解答で
チェック

Step4

覚えておきたい重要語句をチェック
※原則その回での単語の使い方を紹介しています。

Step5

その回で学んだこと・気づいたこと
をメモ

Step6

ビデオ講義で解説を見る　※ビデオ講義の詳細は7ページをご覧ください。

Let's Read!

目　次

たくや先生の紹介

藤井　拓哉（ふじい　たくや）

1984年生まれ。父親の仕事の都合で3歳〜6歳までと、15歳〜24歳までをアメリカのオハイオ州で過ごす。オハイオ州立大学、同大学院で教育学を学び、日本語の教員免許とTESOL（英語を母国語としない方のための英語教授法）を取得。帰国後は、宇都宮大学で英語講師を務める。数学、化学、生物学、物理学を英語で学ぶ「理数系英語」の講義を定期的に行い、2010年と2013年にベストレクチャー賞を受賞。現在は、筑波技術大学で英語講師を務める。著書に『たくや式中学英語ノート』シリーズ全10巻、『たくや式どんどん読める中学英語長文』シリーズ（どちらも朝日学生新聞社）、『MP3CD付き　ガチトレ　英語スピーキング徹底トレーニング』シリーズ（ベレ出版）。TOEIC955点、TOEFL101点。
https://withyoufujii.com　ツイッター：@gachitore1

ビデオ講義の見方

　この本は、たくや先生が全ての問題を解説するビデオ講義を見ながら学ぶことができます。発音をチェックしたり、音読の練習をしたりするのにもお使いください。

※制作の都合によりビデオ講義は2021年9月頃より順次公開予定です。ご了承ください。

❶　「朝日学生新聞社の本」のホームページ〝あさがく・ジェーピー〟
www.asagaku.jpにアクセス。

❷　あさがく・ジェーピーのトップ画面にある「音声講義・ビデオ講義」をクリック。

❸　「たくや式　どんどん読める　中学英語長文4」をクリック

❹　見たい講義をクリック
　　YouTubeにも同じ動画を公開しています。**書名で検索してください。**

【ご注意】
・標準的なパソコン・タブレット・スマートフォンであれば視聴可能ですが、古い型や特殊な設定の端末では再生できない場合があります。判断がつきかねる場合は、まず上記サイトで動画が見られるかどうかご確認ください。
・保守・点検のために、予告なしに一時的に配信を中断することがあります。
・本書の絶版後3年が経過した時には順次配信を停止します。

基礎力確認テスト

Let's Read! 読んでみよう

グレース（Grace）とサツキ（Satsuki）が大学のカフェテリアで話をしています。会話文を読み、後の問題に答えていきましょう。

Satsuki:	Hey, Grace. What's going on?
Grace:	Hi, Satsuki. Did you just get here?
Satsuki:	No. I had a class from 10:30, so I came here around 10:20. I was planning (A) here around 9:30 because I wanted to borrow some books from the library before class, but the roads were very crowded, so it took an hour and a half for me to get here.
Grace:	Do you come to school by car every day?
Satsuki:	Yeah. It is my mother's car, but I use it every day because she uses it only for (B) on weekends. Did you have any classes in the morning?
Grace:	No, I didn't.
Satsuki:	So, what were you (C)?
Grace:	Well, I was practicing the piano until 11 o'clock. I began (D) at 9 o'clock, so it was pretty long. Practicing for two hours without (E) a break was very hard.
Satsuki:	Wow. Why did you need to practice that long?
Grace:	Because I'm in a music band, and we are going to have a concert at Sakura Hall next month. We held a concert last year, too, and it was very good. I think many people enjoyed listening to our music.
Satsuki:	Were there a lot of people at the concert?
Grace:	Yes, there were. (1)(<u>多くの人は立っていたんだ。なぜなら、十分な数の席がなかったから</u>)
Satsuki:	Wow. I see.
Grace:	Oh, I have a question. Will you have time on December 26th? It is Friday and the last day of school before the winter break.
Satsuki:	I think so. I will have time after my math class. It starts at 1:00 and ends at 2:30, so I think I will have time after that. Why?

Grace:	Well, because I'm looking for someone to help me. It is the day before our concert, and we are planning to take all our instruments there on that day. My job is to take eight guitars to the concert hall, and they are not mine. They are big and heavy, so I want to take them by car, but I don't have a car. Will you help me?
Satsuki:	Of course. Do you want me to take the guitars to Sakura Hall?
Grace:	Yes.
Satsuki:	OK. I think I can do that, but my car is very small, so it won't have enough space for you to ride.
Grace:	That's OK. I can take a train and walk to the concert hall.
Satsuki:	OK. Where is the concert hall?
Grace:	It is on Kasama Street. Do you know the park near the station? Sakura Hall is in front of the park. I think there is a parking area behind the concert hall, so you will be able to park your car there.
Satsuki:	Which park are you talking about? Are you talking about Fujishiro Park?
Grace:	No. Not that one. Fujishiro Park is on Tomei Street and a little bit far from the station. I think the name of the park is Motegi Park, but I am not sure. It is big, so you won't miss it.
Satsuki:	Will you draw a map?
Grace:	Sure. That's a good idea. Do you have a piece of paper and a pen?
Satsuki:	Yes, I do. You can use this one.
Grace:	Thanks.
	(5 minutes later)
Grace:	OK. This is the (2)map. It is very easy to get there from the station. Oh, wait. You need to take (3)this.
Satsuki:	What is it?
Grace:	It is a ticket to park your car. You cannot park your car without this ticket.
Satsuki:	OK. Thank you. What time do you want me to pick up the guitars?
Grace:	Let's see. I have a meeting from 2:00, and it is an hour long, so can we meet at 3:30?
Satsuki:	Sounds good. Where do you want me to meet you?
Grace:	Let's meet in front of Building C. I can take you to our practice room from there.
Satsuki:	OK. Sounds good. Oh, sorry. It's time for me to go to class. See you.

Grace:	OK. Enjoy your class.
	(on December 26th)
Satsuki:	Hello, Grace.
Grace:	Hi, Satsuki. Thank you for helping me today. OK. Let's go to the practice room.
Satsuki:	Is it far from here?
Grace:	No, it's not. I think it will only take about two minutes to get there, but it is hard to explain because you need to make many turns.
	(in the practice room)
Grace:	OK. These are (4)the guitars. Can you start taking them to your car? After you finish, you can go to the concert hall. I hope to see you in the parking area.
Satsuki:	Sounds good. Do you want me to take this black guitar, too?
Grace:	No. It's OK. We decided not to use it, so I want you to take these seven guitars.
Satsuki:	Got it.

問 題

Q1. （A）～（E）に入る適切な単語をそれぞれ1つずつ選びましょう。

　　（A）coming / to come / came　　　　（B）shopped / shopping / to shop

　　（C）did / to do / doing　　　　（D）to practice / practiced / to practicing

　　（E）took / taking / tooking

Q2. How long did it take for Satsuki to come to school?

　　1. 30 minutes　　　　2. 45 minutes　　　　3. 60 minutes　　　　4. 90 minutes

Q3. Why did Grace need to practice the piano?

Q4. 下線部 (1) の日本語に合うように、次の空欄に適切な語を入れましょう。

（　　　　　　　　　）people（　　　　　　　　　　）standing because（　　　　　　　　）

（　　　　　　　　　）enough seats.

Q5. なぜグレースはサツキに12月26日に時間があるかたずねたのか、次の中から1つ選びましょう。
1. サツキの数学の授業について質問があったから。
2. 金曜日なので、授業の後でコンサートを見に行きたいと思ったから。
3. 楽器をコンサートホールに持って行かないといけなかったから。
4. サツキの車を運転したいと思ったから。

Q6. 下線部 (2) のmapは、次のうちどれでしょう。

1.
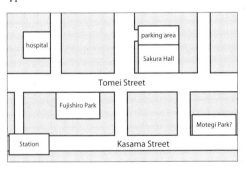

2.
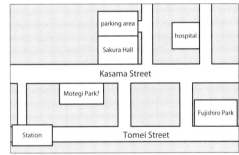

3.
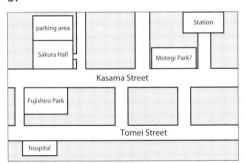

4.
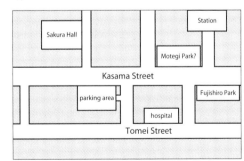

Q7. 下線部 (3) のthisは何か、次の中から1つ選びましょう。
1. ギターを受け取るためのチケット
2. 駐車場に車を止めるためのチケット
3. コンサート会場に入るためのチケット
4. C棟に入るためのチケット

Q8. 下線部 (4) の the guitars は合計何本あったか日本語で答えましょう。

_____

Q9. 12月26日のグレースとサツキの会話が終わった後、彼女たちは次にどこで会う予定となっているか日本語で答えましょう。

_____

Q10. 本文の内容と<u>異なるもの</u>を1つ選びましょう。
1. サツキは毎日車で学校に通っている。
2. グレースたちのコンサートは12月27日に行われる。
3. グレースたちが日頃練習している部屋はC棟からは遠い。
4. 12月26日にサツキは数学の授業がある。

全文の和訳を書いていきましょう。またビデオ講義を使って音読の練習も行っていきましょう。

1.　*Satsuki*:　Hey, Grace. What's going on?

　　サツキ：　_____

2.　*Grace*:　Hi, Satsuki. Did you just get here?

　　グレース：　_____

3.　*Satsuki*:　No. I had a class from 10:30, so I came here around 10:20.

　　サツキ：　_____

4.　　　　I was planning to come here around 9:30 because I wanted to borrow some books from the library before class, but the roads were very crowded, so it took an hour and a half for me to get here.

　　_____

　　_____

　　_____

5.　*Grace*:　Do you come to school by car every day?

　　グレース：　_____

6.　*Satsuki*:　Yeah. It is my mother's car, but I use it every day because she uses it only for shopping on weekends.

　　サツキ：　_____

7.   Did you have any classes in the morning?

_____

8.   *Grace*:   No, I didn't.

    グレース： _____

9.   *Satsuki*:   So, what were you doing?

    サツキ： _____

10.   *Grace*:   Well, I was practicing the piano until 11 o'clock.

    グレース： _____

11.   I began to practice at 9 o'clock, so it was pretty long.

_____

12.   Practicing for two hours without taking a break was very hard.

_____

13.   *Satsuki*:   Wow. Why did you need to practice that long?

    サツキ： _____

14.   *Grace*:   Because I'm in a music band, and we are going to have a concert at Sakura Hall next month.

    グレース： _____

15.   We held a concert last year, too, and it was very good.

_____

16.　　　　　　　I think many people enjoyed listening to our music.

_____

17.　*Satsuki*:　Were there a lot of people at the concert?

　　　サツキ:　_____

18.　*Grace*:　Yes, there were.

　　　グレース:　_____

19.　　　　　　　Many people were standing because there weren't enough seats.

_____

20.　*Satsuki*:　Wow. I see.

　　　サツキ:　_____

21.　*Grace*:　Oh, I have a question. Will you have time on December 26th?

　　　グレース:　_____

22.　　　　　　　It is Friday and the last day of school before the winter break.

_____

23.　*Satsuki*:　I think so. I will have time after my math class.

　　　サツキ:　_____

24.　　　　　　　It starts at 1:00 and ends at 2:30, so I think I will have time after that. Why?

_____

25. *Grace*: Well, because I'm looking for someone to help me.

グレース： _____

26. It is the day before our concert, and we are planning to take all our instruments there on that day.

_____

_____

27. My job is to take eight guitars to the concert hall, and they are not mine.

_____

28. They are big and heavy, so I want to take them by car, but I don't have a car. Will you help me?

_____

_____

29. *Satsuki*: Of course. Do you want me to take the guitars to Sakura Hall?

サツキ： _____

30. *Grace*: Yes.

グレース： _____

31. *Satsuki*: OK. I think I can do that, but my car is very small, so it won't have enough space for you to ride.

サツキ： _____

32. *Grace*: That's OK. I can take a train and walk to the concert hall.

グレース： _____

33. *Satsuki*: OK. Where is the concert hall?

サツキ： _____

34. *Grace*: It is on Kasama Street. Do you know the park near the station?

グレース： _____

35. Sakura Hall is in front of the park.

_____

36. I think there is a parking area behind the concert hall, so you will be able to park your car there.

_____

37. *Satsuki*: Which park are you talking about?

サツキ： _____

38. Are you talking about Fujishiro Park?

_____

39. *Grace*: No. Not that one.

グレース： _____

40. Fujishiro Park is on Tomei Street and a little bit far from the station.

_____

41.   I think the name of the park is Motegi Park, but I am not sure.

_____

42.   It is big, so you won't miss it.

_____

43.   *Satsuki*: Will you draw a map?

サツキ： _____

44.   *Grace*: Sure. That's a good idea. Do you have a piece of paper and a pen?

グレース： _____

45.   *Satsuki*: Yes, I do. You can use this one.

サツキ： _____

46.   *Grace*: Thanks.

グレース： _____

(5 minutes later) (5分後)

47.   *Grace*: OK. This is the map. It is very easy to get there from the station.

グレース： _____

48.   Oh, wait. You need to take this.

_____

49. *Satsuki*:　What is it?

サツキ：　_____

50. *Grace*:　It is a ticket to park your car.

グレース：　_____

51.　You cannot park your car without this ticket.

_____

52. *Satsuki*:　OK. Thank you. What time do you want me to pick up the guitars?

サツキ：　_____

53. *Grace*:　Let's see. I have a meeting from 2:00, and it is an hour long, so can we meet at 3:30?

グレース：　_____

_____

54. *Satsuki*:　Sounds good. Where do you want me to meet you?

サツキ：　_____

55. *Grace*:　Let's meet in front of Building C.

グレース：　_____

56.　I can take you to our practice room from there.

_____

57. *Satsuki*: OK. Sounds good. Oh, sorry. It's time for me to go to class. See you.

サツキ：　_____

58. *Grace*: OK. Enjoy your class.

グレース：　_____

(on December 26th) (12月26日)

59. *Satsuki*: Hello, Grace.

サツキ：　_____

60. *Grace*: Hi, Satsuki. Thank you for helping me today.

グレース：　_____

61. OK. Let's go to the practice room.

_____

62. *Satsuki*: Is it far from here?

サツキ：　_____

63. *Grace*: No, it's not. I think it will only take about two minutes to get there, but it is hard to explain because you need to make many turns.

グレース：　_____

_____

(in the practice room) (練習部屋にて)

64. *Grace*: OK. These are the guitars. Can you start taking them to your car?

    グレース: _____

65. After you finish, you can go to the concert hall.

    _____

66. I hope to see you in the parking area.

    _____

67. *Satsuki*: Sounds good. Do you want me to take this black guitar, too?

    サツキ: _____

68. *Grace*: No. It's OK.

    グレース: _____

69. We decided not to use it, so I want you to take these seven guitars.

    _____

70. *Satsuki*: Got it.

    サツキ: _____

新しい助動詞

会社員のエマ（Emma）とジョン（John）が、昼食について オフィスで話をしています。やりとりを読み、後の 問題に答えていきましょう。

Emma:	Hey, John. Where do you want to go for lunch today?
John:	I don't know. Where did we go yesterday?
Emma:	It was the curry restaurant on the Main Street. I forgot the name, but we go there a lot.
John:	Oh, it's (1)Curry-Go-Go.
Emma:	That's right. I have to write it somewhere because I cannot remember it. I want to take my family there sometime because their curry is good, and it comes with a lot of salad and *naan.
John:	Yeah. I know. You should do that. I am sure your family will love it. Last weekend, I went there with my wife, and she really enjoyed the curry.
Emma:	Could she finish all the food?
John:	No, she couldn't. It was too much food for her. Anyway, so let's not go to Curry-Go-Go today.
Emma:	OK. Where should we go? We go out for lunch every day, so we may not have many new choices.
John:	Let's see. How about Olio? It is an Italian restaurant near Akatsuka Gym. It is a little bit far from here, but their pizza is very good. I think we can come back by one o'clock. What do you think?
Emma:	Yes. That sounds good. Oh, wait. We cannot go to that restaurant because I have a meeting from one. I forgot about that. I'm sorry.
John:	What time do you want to come back?
Emma:	I want to come back here by 12:50 because I may need some time to prepare.
John:	OK. We must choose a restaurant quickly then. Let me look some up. (looking up some restaurants on the computer)
John:	How about this one? It is a family restaurant near Inaba Park. It is only

300 meters away from here.

Emma: I didn't know we had a family restaurant around here. What is the name?

John: It's Jyo-Jyo. It is a new restaurant. This website says it opened only a month ago, but look at all these positive comments.

Emma: Oh, my gosh. I cannot believe it. (2)<u>They must serve very good food</u>. I hope it is not crowded.

John: It is raining outside. Should we go by car?

Emma: Sure. I don't want to walk in the rain. Let's go by car.

(at the restaurant)

Emma: Wow. We are lucky. There are not that many people here today.

John: I know. The weather is not nice, maybe that's why.

Waiter: May I help you?

Emma: Oh, yes. Is this the waiting list? Do I have to write my name here?

Waiter: Could you wait for a second? (ア   ) Oh, you don't have to write your name. How many people?

Emma: Just two.

Waiter: Smoking or non-smoking?

Emma: Non-smoking please.

Waiter: OK. Follow me please.

John: I thought you smoked.

Emma: Well, I do, but I don't think we have enough time to enjoy smoking after lunch today.

(at the table)

Emma: This table is nice. I like this big window because I can see outside. It is close to the kitchen, too.

John: Right. Let's see the menu.... Wow. Everything looks very delicious.

Emma: Remember. We must eat very quickly.

Waiter: May I take your orders?

Emma: Well, I need your help. We do not have much time because we need to leave here in 30 minutes. And I don't want to eat soup or noodles because I may get a *stain. I don't want to eat garlic, either, because I have a meeting this afternoon. Oh, and no curry because I had one yesterday. So what should I eat?

Waiter: How about our *grilled salmon? I think we can prepare this within 10 minutes. It comes with salad, a drink, and a dessert. And it is only 800 yen.

Emma:	That sounds good. I will have that.
John:	It does sound good. I'll have that, too.
Waiter:	OK. What do you want for drink and dessert? The list is on the back of the menu.
Emma:	I will have coffee and *vanilla ice cream for my dessert.
John:	I'll have the same.
	(The waiter is gone.)
John:	What are you reading?
Emma:	Oh, this? I have to explain many things during the meeting today, and this is the list. I must remember them because I must not look at the memo when I explain these things.
John:	Why not?
Emma:	Well, because my boss says so. I looked at the memo and talked about our schedule last time, and my boss didn't like it. He thinks I should stand up straight and talk clearly. I do agree with him, but it is very difficult for me to do it. I am checking the list right now, but I think I will get nervous and forget everything, so (3)this may not help me at all.
	(The waiter brings the dishes.)
Waiter:	OK. Here you go.
John:	Thank you. It looks great.
Waiter:	I will bring your desserts after you finish your meals. Do you see that button on the table? You can press that to let me know. Enjoy your meals.
Emma & John:	Thank you.
	(They finished eating.)
John:	I'm done. It was very good. I really liked the salmon and the dessert. We should come here again.
Emma:	I know. I liked the dessert. The ice cream was very good. OK. What time is it?
John:	It is 12:45, so we need to go back now. Shall we?
Emma:	Sure.

* naan ナン（インド・西アジアなどの平たいパン）　　stain しみ/よごれ　　grilled グリルされた/調理された
vanilla バニラ

Q1. 下線部 (1) の Curry-Go-Go について会話文に書かれているものには○、書かれていないものには×を（　）に書きましょう。

1. ジョンとエマはよく行く。（　　）

2. アカツカ体育館の近くにある。（　　）

3. エマは家族を連れて行きたいと考えている。（　　）

4. 最近オープンした。（　　）

Q2. 今回、ジョンとエマが昼食にオリオ（Olio）に行けない理由を日本語で答えましょう。

_____

Q3. エマが下線部 (2) と発言した理由を日本語で答えましょう。

_____

Q4. Why did John and Emma decide to go to the restaurant by car?

Because _____.

Q5. （ア）に入る最も適切な文を1つ選びましょう。

1. You could not come here yesterday.

2. I'm sorry. We don't have any open seats.

3. I need to check the tables.

4. Could you park your car?

Q6. ジョンとエマがレストランで通された席に一番近いのは、次のうちどれでしょう。

1.
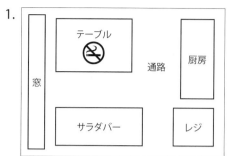

2.
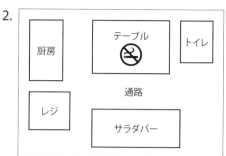

3.
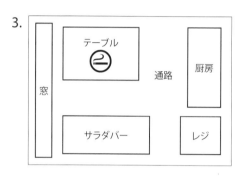

4.
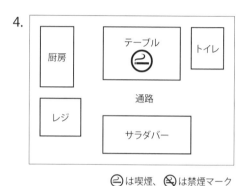

は喫煙、は禁煙マーク

Q7. エマが焼き鮭（grilled salmon）を選んだ理由に当てはまらないものを、1つ選びましょう。

1. ニンニクを使っていない。　　　2. すぐに用意できる。

3. 汁などが飛び跳ねない。　　　　4. 肉は食べたくなかった。

Q8. 下線部（3）のthisは何を指すか日本語で答えましょう。

Q9. What do Emma and John need to do to get their desserts after their meals?

Q10. 次のうち本文には書かれていないものを1つ選びましょう。

1. エマはタバコを吸う。

2. ジョンはオリオ（Olio）に家族を連れていきたいと思っている。

3. ジョンはデザートにバニラアイスを頼んだ。

4. ジョージョー（Jyo-Jyo）は、ジョンとエマのオフィスに近い。

　助動詞とは、canのように動詞だけでは表すことのできない可能・必然・義務・意思などの意味を表す単語です。肯定文/否定文/疑問文の形は、基本的にcanの文章と同じなので、そこまで複雑ではないのですが、疑問文にすると意味が多少変わる助動詞もあります。今回登場する助動詞は should / must / *have to / could / may / **shall の6つです。

* have to は一般動詞の文となりますが、助動詞の役割を果たします。
** shall は疑問文のみ登場です。

1. 助動詞の文の基本的な形*

【肯定文】　主語 ＋ 助動詞 ＋ 動詞 ＋ 〜.

【否定文】　主語 ＋ 助動詞 not ＋ 動詞 ＋ 〜.

【疑問文】　助動詞 ＋ 主語 ＋ 動詞 ＋ 〜?

【疑問詞のつく疑問文】　疑問詞 ＋ 助動詞 ＋ 主語 ＋ 動詞 ＋ 〜?

* have toは一般動詞の文となるので、少し形が異なります。

2. 今回登場する助動詞の意味

（1）should

【肯定文】　〜すべき

　　　　　He should go home now. （彼は今家に帰るべきです）

【否定文】　〜すべきではない

　　　　　He should not (shouldn't) go home now. （彼は今家に帰るべきではないです）

【疑問文】　〜すべきですか

　　　　　Why should he go home now? （なぜ彼は今家に帰るべきなのですか）

（2）must

【肯定文】　〜しなくてはならない (have toと同じ意味) / 〜に違いない

　　　　　He must do this. （彼はこれをしなくてはいけません）

　　　　　She must know the answer. （彼女は答えを知っているに違いない）

【否定文】　〜してはいけない (may notよりも強い禁止)

　　　　　You must not (mustn't) come with me. （あなたは私と一緒に来てはいけません）

【疑問文】　〜しないといけないのですか

　　　　　Must I eat this salad? （私はこのサラダを食べないといけないのですか）

(3) have to

【肯定文】 ～しなくてはならない（mustと同じ意味）

You have to go to school. （あなたは学校に行かないといけません）

【否定文】 ～しなくてもよい

She did not (didn't) have to write this.

（彼女はこれを書かなくてもよかったです）

【疑問文】 ～しないといけないのですか（Must ～?と同じ意味）

Why does he have to buy it? （なぜ彼はそれを買わないといけないのですか）

> **＋プラス1** **mustとhave toの肯定文の使い分け**
>
> 基本的にmustとhave toは同じ使い方をするのですがmustは過去形や未来形にすることができません。そのため、「～しないといけませんでした」と言いたい場合は、have toの過去形had toを使い、「～しないといけなくなるでしょう」と未来のことを言いたい場合はwill have toを使います。

(4) could

【肯定文】 ～できた（canの過去形）

She could run very fast. （彼女はとても速く走れました）

【否定文】 ～できなかった（cannotの過去形）

I could not (couldn't) finish it. （私は、それを終わらせられなかったです）

【疑問文】 ～できましたか（Can ～?の過去形）

Could he go to school? （彼は学校に行けたのですか）

> **＋プラス1** **Could you ～?はCan you ～?の丁寧な言い方**
>
> Could you ～?は「～していただけますか」という意味でもよく使われます（Can you ～?の丁寧な言い方）。英語では現在のことでも過去形を用いて表現することで、ニュアンスを和らげることができます（過去形を用いることで現実から距離を置くことができ、直接的な表現でなくなる）。そのため、ここでも過去形が使われるのです。
>
> 〈例〉 Could you open the window? （窓を開けていただけますか）

（5）may

【肯定文】　～してもよい（can の丁寧な言い方）/ ～かもしれない

You may start the test.　（あなたはテストを始めてもよいです）

She may come today.　（彼女は今日来るかもしれません）

【否定文】　～することはできない（cannot の丁寧な言い方）/ ～でないかもしれない

You *may not leave the room.　（あなたは部屋を出ることはできません）

He may not like this.　（彼はこれが好きではないかもしれません）

＊ may not の省略形はない。

【疑問文】　～してもよいですか（May I ～? の形でよく使われる。Can I ～? の丁寧な言い方）

May I use your computer?　（あなたのパソコンを使ってもよいですか）

（6）Shall

【疑問文】　～しましょうか（Shall（I / We）～? の形でよく使われる）

Shall we do this together?　（これを一緒にやりましょうか）

＋プラス1　**現在はあまり使われない "Shall ～?"**

　一般的に "Shall ～?" は、古い言い方のため、現在はあまり使われていません。代わりに "Do you want me to ～?" "Let's ～." "Should ～?"（should は「～しましょうか」という意味でも使われる）の形がよく使われます。参考程度に覚えておきましょう。

〈例〉　ドアをしめましょうか。

Shall I close the door?　→　Do you want me to close the door?

　　　　　　　　　　　　　→　Should I close the door?

図書館に行きましょうか。

Shall we go to the library?　→　Let's go to the library.

　　　　　　　　　　　　　　→　Should we go to the library?

---

3. 疑問文の答え方は臨機応変に

　今回登場する助動詞の疑問文では、同じ助動詞では答えないものもあります。なぜなら、同じ疑問文を使って答えると少し意味の違った答えになってしまうからです。ポイントは「疑問文の意図や目的を想像する」こと。機械的に「助動詞で質問されたから、同じ助動詞で答える」のではなく、一つひとつ「どういう答えが求められているのか?」を考えていきましょう。

〈例〉Must I practice the guitar?　（私はギターを練習しないといけないのですか）

No, you must not.　（いいえ、してはいけません）　　　　＝ ×

No, you don't have to.　（いいえ、しなくてもよいです）　＝ ○

【同じ助動詞で答えられる疑問文】

(1) Should〜？ ＝ 〜すべきですか

　　〈例〉Should I write my name here? （私の名前をここに書くべきですか）

　　　　　Yes, you should. / No, you shouldn't.

　　　　　（はい、するべきです／いいえ、するべきではないです）

(2) Do 〜 have to〜？ ＝ 〜しないといけませんか

　　〈例〉Do I have to go there? （私はそこに行かないといけないのですか）

　　　　　Yes, you do. / No, you don't. （はい、そうです／いいえ、行かなくてもよいです）

(3) Could〜？（Can〜？の過去形）＝ 〜できましたか

　　〈例〉Could he pass the test? （彼はテストに合格できたのですか）

　　　　　Yes, he could. / No, he couldn't. （はい、できました／いいえ、できませんでした）

【同じ助動詞で答えられない疑問文（答え方をいくつか紹介）】

(1) Must〜？ ＝ 〜しないといけませんか

　　はい　　→　Yes, 〜must. （はい、そうです）

　　いいえ　→　No, 〜don't have to. （いいえ、しなくてもよいです）

　　　　　　→　No, 〜don't need to. （いいえ、する必要はないです）

　　　　　　→　That's OK. （それは大丈夫です）　など

> （注）No, you must not. とすると「してはいけません」になるので注意。

　　〈例〉Must she buy this textbook? （彼女はこの教科書を買わないといけないのですか）

　　　　　Yes, she must. / No, she doesn't have to.

(2) Could 〜？ ＝ 〜していただけますか

　　はい　　→　Sure. （もちろん）

　　　　　　→　Of course. （もちろん）　など

　　いいえ　→　No, I can't. （いいえ、できません）

　　　　　　→　I'm sorry. I can't. （ごめんなさい、できません）　など

　　〈例〉Could you open the door? （ドアを開けていただけますか）

　　　　　Sure. / I'm sorry. I can't.

(3) May I ～? ＝ ～してもよいですか

はい　　→　Yes, you can.（はい、よいですよ）

　　　　→　Sure.（もちろん）　など

いいえ　→　I'm sorry. You can't.（ごめんなさい。できません）　など

> （注）Yes, you may や No, you may not. と答えることも可能だが、目上の人が目下の人に使うようなぶっきらぼうな表現になるので注意。

〈例〉May I sit here?（ここに座ってもいいですか）

　　　 Yes, you can. / I'm sorry. You can't.

(4) Shall I ～? ＝ ～しましょうか

はい　　→　Yes, please.（はい、お願いします）

　　　　→　Yes, thank you.（はい、ありがとう）　など

> （注）Yes, you shall. という表現は、ほとんど使われない。

いいえ　→　No, thanks.（いいです、ありがとう）

　　　　→　That's all right.（それは大丈夫です）　など

〈例〉Shall I close the door?（窓を閉めましょうか）

　　　 Yes, please. / That's all right.

(5) Shall we ～? ＝ ～しましょうよ

はい　　→　Yes (, let's).（はい、そうしましょう）

　　　　→　Sure.（もちろん）　など

いいえ　→　No (, let's not).（いいえ、やめておきましょう）

　　　　→　That's all right.（それは大丈夫です）　など

〈例〉Shall we do this now?（今、これをしましょうよ）

　　　 Sure. / No, let's not.

＋プラス1　強調で使われる do / does / did

　専門的なことですが、一般動詞の疑問文や否定文で登場する do / does / did の品詞は助動詞です。しかし、一般的な助動詞とは使い方が少し異なりますので「助動詞」であることをあまり意識する必要はありません。また、助動詞の do / does / did は肯定文でも使うことができます。例えば、"I do need this." という形で使うことができます。これは、動詞を「強調」する時に使われます。

〈例〉I do need this.（私は、これが本当に必要です）

　　　I did *clean up my room.（私は、ちゃんと部屋を掃除しました）

　　　　　　　　　　　　＊ did が入っているので、一般動詞は現在形が使われる。

この「強調」で使われる do / does / did はよく登場するので覚えておきましょう。

全文の和訳を書いていきましょう。またビデオ講義を
使って音読の練習も行っていきましょう。

1.　*Emma*:　　Hey, John. Where do you want to go for lunch today?

　　エマ:　　_____

2.　*John*:　　I don't know. Where did we go yesterday?

　　ジョン:　　_____

3.　*Emma*:　　It was the curry restaurant on the Main Street.

　　エマ:　　_____

4.　　　　　I forgot the name, but we go there a lot.

　　　　　　_____

5.　*John*:　　Oh, it's Curry-Go-Go.

　　ジョン:　　_____

6.　*Emma*:　　That's right. I have to write it somewhere because I cannot remember it.

　　エマ:　　_____

7.　　　　　I want to take my family there sometime because their curry is good,
　　　　　　and it comes with a lot of salad and naan.

　　　　　　_____

　　　　　　_____

8.　*John*:　Yeah. I know. You should do that. I am sure your family will love it.

　　ジョン：　_____

9.　　　　　Last weekend, I went there with my wife, and she really enjoyed the curry.

　　　　　_____

　　　　　_____

10.　*Emma*:　Could she finish all the food?

　　エマ：　_____

11.　*John*:　No, she couldn't. It was too much food for her.

　　ジョン：　_____

12.　　　　　Anyway, so let's not go to Curry-Go-Go today.

　　　　　_____

13.　*Emma*:　OK. Where should we go?

　　エマ：　_____

14.　　　　　We go out for lunch every day, so we may not have many new choices.

　　　　　_____

15.　*John*:　Let's see. How about Olio?

　　ジョン：　_____

16.   It is an Italian restaurant near Akatsuka Gym.

_____

17.   It is a little bit far from here, but their pizza is very good.

_____

18.   I think we can come back by one o'clock. What do you think?

_____

19.   *Emma*:   Yes. That sounds good. Oh, wait.

     エマ: _____

20.   We cannot go to that restaurant because I have a meeting from one.

_____

21.   I forgot about that. I'm sorry.

_____

22.   *John*:   What time do you want to come back?

   ジョン: _____

23.   *Emma*:   I want to come back here by 12:50 because I may need some time to prepare.

     エマ: _____

_____

24. *John*: OK. We must choose a restaurant quickly then. Let me look some up.

　ジョン： _____

(looking up some restaurants on the computer)
(パソコンでいくつかのレストランを調べている)

25. *John*: How about this one? It is a family restaurant near Inaba Park.

　ジョン： _____

26. It is only 300 meters away from here.

_____

27. *Emma*: I didn't know we had a family restaurant around here.

　エマ： _____

28. What is the name?

_____

29. *John*: It's Jyo-Jyo. It is a new restaurant. This website says it opened only a month ago, but look at all these positive comments.

　ジョン： _____

_____

30. *Emma*: Oh, my gosh. I cannot believe it. They must serve very good food.

　エマ： _____

31.   I hope it is not crowded.

_____

32.   *John*:   It is raining outside. Should we go by car?

     ジョン: _____

33.   *Emma*:   Sure. I don't want to walk in the rain. Let's go by car.

     エマ: _____

          (at the restaurant) (レストランにて)

34.   *Emma*:   Wow. We are lucky. There are not that many people here today.

     エマ: _____

35.   *John*:   I know. The weather is not nice, maybe that's why.

     ジョン: _____

36.   *Waiter*: May I help you?

     ウェイター: _____

37.   *Emma*:   Oh, yes. Is this the waiting list? Do I have to write my name here?

     エマ: _____

38.   *Waiter*: Could you wait for a second? I need to check the tables.

     ウェイター: _____

39.   Oh, you don't have to write your name. How many people?

_____

40.   *Emma*:   Just two.

    エマ: _____

41.   *Waiter*:   Smoking or non-smoking?

    ウェイター: _____

42.   *Emma*:   Non-smoking please.

    エマ: _____

43.   *Waiter*:   OK. Follow me please.

    ウェイター: _____

44.   *John*:   I thought you smoked.

    ジョン: _____

45.   *Emma*:   Well, I do, but I don't think we have enough time to enjoy smoking after lunch today.

    エマ: _____

_____

    (at the table) (テーブルにて)

46.   *Emma*:   This table is nice. I like this big window because I can see outside.

    エマ: _____

47. It is close to the kitchen, too.

_____

48. *John*: Right. Let's see the menu.... Wow. Everything looks very delicious.

ジョン: _____

49. *Emma*: Remember. We must eat very quickly.

エマ: _____

50. *Waiter*: May I take your orders?

ウェイター: _____

51. *Emma*: Well, I need your help. We do not have much time because we need to leave here in 30 minutes.

エマ: _____

_____

52. And I don't want to eat soup or noodles because I may get a stain.

_____

53. I don't want to eat garlic, either, because I have a meeting this afternoon.

_____

54. Oh, and no curry because I had one yesterday. So what should I eat?

_____

55. *Waiter*: How about our grilled salmon?

    ウェイター: ＿＿＿＿＿＿＿＿＿＿＿＿＿＿＿＿＿＿＿＿＿＿＿＿＿＿

56. I think we can prepare this within 10 minutes.

    ＿＿＿＿＿＿＿＿＿＿＿＿＿＿＿＿＿＿＿＿＿＿＿＿＿＿

57. It comes with salad, a drink, and a dessert. And it is only 800 yen.

    ＿＿＿＿＿＿＿＿＿＿＿＿＿＿＿＿＿＿＿＿＿＿＿＿＿＿

58. *Emma*: That sounds good. I will have that.

    エマ: ＿＿＿＿＿＿＿＿＿＿＿＿＿＿＿＿＿＿＿＿＿＿＿＿＿＿

59. *John*: It does sound good. I'll have that, too.

    ジョン: ＿＿＿＿＿＿＿＿＿＿＿＿＿＿＿＿＿＿＿＿＿＿＿＿＿＿

60. *Waiter*: OK. What do you want for drink and dessert?

    ウェイター: ＿＿＿＿＿＿＿＿＿＿＿＿＿＿＿＿＿＿＿＿＿＿＿＿＿＿

61. The list is on the back of the menu.

    ＿＿＿＿＿＿＿＿＿＿＿＿＿＿＿＿＿＿＿＿＿＿＿＿＿＿

62. *Emma*: I will have coffee and vanilla ice cream for my dessert.

    エマ: ＿＿＿＿＿＿＿＿＿＿＿＿＿＿＿＿＿＿＿＿＿＿＿＿＿＿

63. *John*: I'll have the same.

    ジョン: ＿＿＿＿＿＿＿＿＿＿＿＿＿＿＿＿＿＿＿＿＿＿＿＿＿＿

(The waiter is gone.) (ウェイターが去る)

64. *John*:   What are you reading?

    ジョン: _____

65. *Emma*:   Oh, this? I have to explain many things during the meeting today, and this is the list.

    エマ: _____

    _____

66.   I must remember them because I must not look at the memo when I explain these things.

    _____

    _____

67. *John*:   Why not?

    ジョン: _____

68. *Emma*:   Well, because my boss says so.

    エマ: _____

69.   I looked at the memo and talked about our schedule last time, and my boss didn't like it.

    _____

    _____

70.　　　　　　　He thinks I should stand up straight and talk clearly.

_____

71.　　　　　　　I do agree with him, but it is very difficult for me to do it.

_____

72.　　　　　　　I am checking the list right now, but I think I will get nervous and forget everything, so this may not help me at all.

_____

_____

(The waiter brings the dishes.)（ウェイターが料理を持ってくる）

73.　_Waiter_:　OK. Here you go.

ウェイター：_____

74.　_John_:　Thank you. It looks great.

ジョン：_____

75.　_Waiter_:　I will bring your desserts after you finish your meals.

ウェイター：_____

76.　　　　　　　Do you see that button on the table? You can press that to let me know.

_____

77.　　　　　　　Enjoy your meals.

_____

78. Emma & John: Thank you.

エマ＆ジョン： _____

(They finished eating.) (彼らが食事を終えて)

79. *John*:   I'm done. It was very good. I really liked the salmon and the dessert.

ジョン： _____

80.   We should come here again.

_____

81. *Emma*:   I know. I liked the dessert. The ice cream was very good.

エマ： _____

82.   OK. What time is it?

_____

83. *John*:   It is 12:45, so we need to go back now. Shall we?

ジョン： _____

84. *Emma*:   Sure.

エマ： _____

語句の確認

meal	【名(可算)】食事 / 食事時間
memo	【名(可算)】メモ
*¹back	【名(可算)】背中 / 裏側 / 裏面
salmon	【名(可算)】鮭 【名(不可算)】鮭の肉
choice	【名(不可算)】選択(具体的には可算)
comment	【名(不可算)】コメント / 批評(具体的には可算)
curry	【名(不可算)】(料理名の)カレー料理 / カレー
garlic	【名(不可算)】ニンニク

serve	【動】(食事などを)提供する /(国などに)仕える / 務める
agree(with〜)	【動】(〜に)同意する / 賛成する
somewhere	【副】どこかに / どこかで / どこかへ
sometime	【副】いつか / そのうち
maybe	【副】(通常文頭に置いて)たぶん / もしかすると
*²away	【副】向こうに / 離れて
look〜up / look up〜	【熟】〜を調べる
*³be done	【熟】終わっている

*¹ backは「戻って / 後方へ」という意味の副詞としても使われる。表側 / 表 = front
*² 具体的な距離が「どれだけ離れている」という場合「距離 + away」の形が使われる。
　〈例〉The station is about <u>1km away</u> from my school. 　(駅は、私の学校から約1キロ離れたところにあります)
*³ finishと似たような意味で使われる。「〜が終わる」という場合は、be done with の形が用いられる。
　〈例〉I am done with my homework. 　(私は宿題が終わっている)
　　　〈I finished my homework.と似た意味で使われる〉

まとめを書こう

be動詞の原形と接続詞 if / when / that

次のオンラインの記事を読み、後の問題に答えていきましょう。

Do you want to become a vlogger?

What did you want to be when you were little? Did you want to be a professional baseball player? Or did you want to be a doctor? I wanted to be a singer because I liked to sing in front of people. When I was in elementary school, I saw many *idols on TV, and I wanted to be like them. I went to karaoke with my sister to practice singing. I joined a dance team to practice dancing, too. I think I worked very hard, but I noticed that to be a popular singer was really difficult, so I decided to be something else. But my question was "What do I want to be?" I liked to write when I was in high school. In fact, I had a blog website and enjoyed writing articles, so I decided to be a journalist when I grew up. I studied journalism in college and got a job as a journalist after I graduated. I am happy to be a journalist because writing articles is fun.

What is my point? I want to say that children's dreams may change when they grow up. Why am I saying this? I am saying this because some *surveys done in Japan in 2018 show that many children want to be (1)vloggers when they grow up, and some parents do not think it is a good idea. Who are vloggers? Vloggers are like bloggers, people make money by writing blogs, but vloggers use video. They film themselves and upload their videos on a website to show them to people all over the world. If many people see their videos, they can get money from the website. If you become a popular vlogger, some companies will ask you to *advertise their products, so you will be able to get money by using their products in your videos. A YouTuber is another name for a vlogger because many vloggers upload their videos on YouTube, a popular website to share their videos. Some successful vloggers make 100 million yen or more every year. They live in good houses, drive cool cars, and eat good food.

It sounds like a great job, but why are some parents against it? They are against it because they think living as vloggers is not easy. They don't think just anyone can do it. In fact, many vloggers cannot make enough money to live. They have a different job because they are not getting any money from the website, so they cannot live just by making their own videos. Some people say that becoming a successful vlogger is like becoming a successful actor because vloggers may have to live poorly until they become famous. You need to be creative, too, because you need to make interesting, funny, or unique videos, so people will want to see your videos. If your videos are not good, nobody will see them, and that means your videos will not make any money. In addition, vloggers need to film themselves, edit their videos, and upload them by themselves, and they need to do this every day! In fact, many famous vloggers in Japan upload 400 or more videos every year. That means they make one or more videos every day. They do not have summer or winter vacations. They must work hard when people are taking a break. It is going to be very difficult if their work is not fun.

Some children think that working as a vlogger sounds really good because they can work freely and have fun all the time. Is (2)that true? The answer is "No." Children should know working as a vlogger is hard, but children cannot see that from vloggers' videos, so some parents are worried about that. However, it is not a big problem because children will understand (3)the difficulties when they grow up. In fact, some other surveys done in Japan show that many high schools students think that becoming a vlogger is not *realistic. Many high school students answered that they wanted to become teachers, computer programmers, or engineers instead.

I am not saying that becoming a vlogger is a bad idea, but it is a unique job. If you like filming yourself, editing videos and showing them to the world, I think becoming a vlogger is a great idea. If one of my friends tells me that he or she wants to be a vlogger, I will say (4)go for it because some vloggers are very successful and rich, and he or she may become one of them. If my daughter tells me she wants to be a vlogger, (　ア　) "Are you really sure that you will be able to do this? You may be very poor. You may not have any vacations, either. Do you really think you will be OK?" If she answers "Yes" to these questions, I think I will support her.

---

* idol アイドル　　surveys done in Japan 日本で行われた調査　　advertise 広告する / 宣伝する　　realistic 現実的

問題

Q1.　What did the author want to be when she was a child?

_____

Q2.　What did the author study when she was in college?

_____

Q3.　下線部 (1) のvloggersについて、正しいものには○、間違っているものには×を（　）に
　　　書きましょう。

　　　1. 2018年の時点で、日本の子どもが将来なりたい職業として人気がある。（　　　）

　　　2. 企業にお金を払って、ブログを有名にしている。（　　　）

　　　3. 一部の親は自分の子どもがvloggerになることを反対している。（　　　）

　　　4. 成功者でも、年収は1000万円程度と言われている。（　　　）

Q4.　vloggerの別名を本文中から抜き出しましょう。

_____

Q5.　著者が思う、vloggerとして生きていくのが大変な理由を日本語で2つ書きましょう。

　　　1. _____

　　　2. _____

Q6.　下線部 (2) のthatが指す内容を英語で答えましょう。

_____

_____

Q7.　下線部（3）の the difficulties を詳しく説明するとしたら、以下の（　）に入る単語は何でしょう。

　　　The difficulties of （　　　　　　　　） as a （　　　　　　　　）

Q8.　下線部（4）の go for it の意味は次のうちどれか、1つ選びましょう。
　　　1. 頑張ってみなよ。
　　　2. 行く場所はそこだ。
　　　3. そのために行け。
　　　4. やめておけ。

Q9.　（ア）に入る最も適切な文を1つ選びましょう。
　　　1. I will be able to help her.
　　　2. I will tell her to answer my questions first.
　　　3. I will not be happy about it.
　　　4. she will have to buy a new video camera.

Q10.　次のうち本文の内容とは異なるものを1つ選びましょう。
　　　1. この記事の著者は小さい時にダンスを習っていた。
　　　2. vlogger よりも、教員やエンジニアになりたい高校生の方が日本には多い。
　　　3. 著者には vlogger になりたい娘がいる。
　　　4. 日本には1年で400本以上の動画を上げる vlogger がいる。

be動詞の原形beには、様々な使い方があるのですが、ここでは「助動詞 + be」や「to + be」の形を学んでいきます。基本的にはbe動詞の文に「助動詞」や「toの入ったフレーズ（want toなど）」を足したい時に使われます。また、今回は3つの接続詞if / when / thatについても確認していきます。

1. 「助動詞 + be」「to + be」の形で使われるbe

beは、be動詞の文に「助動詞」や「toの入ったフレーズ（want toなど）」を足したい時に使わます。その理由は、**助動詞やtoの後には動詞の原形が必要**だからです。

〈例〉They are late. （彼らは遅れています）

     ↓   willを足す場合

They **will be** late. （彼らは遅れるでしょう）

(They will <u>are</u> late. ＝ ×)

He is an English teacher. （彼は英語の先生です）

     ↓   want toを足す場合

He **wants to be** an English teacher. （彼は英語の先生になりたいです）

(He wants to <u>is</u> an English teacher. ＝ ×)

また否定文や疑問文の形は、文全体が何の文なのか（一般動詞の文？ 助動詞の文？）によって決まります。

〈例〉<u>They will be late.</u> ＝ 助動詞（will）の文

   否定文：They **will not** be late. （彼らは遅れないでしょう）

   疑問文：**Will** they be late? （彼らは遅れる予定ですか）

<u>He wants to be an English teacher.</u> ＝ 一般動詞の文

   否定文：He **does not** want to be an English teacher.

       （彼は英語の先生になりたくありません）

   疑問文：**Does** he want to be an English teacher?

       （彼は英語の先生になりたいのですか）

2.　接続詞の if / when / that

（1）if ＝ もし〜なら（仮定法）

【肯定文・否定文】

①If A, B　→　もし A なら、B　＊通常 A の後にカンマ（,）を打つ

　　〈例〉If you want to go to college, you need to study more.

　　　　（もしあなたが大学に行きたいのなら、あなたはもっと勉強する必要があります）

②A if B　→　A、もし B なら　＊①のように訳される場合もある

　　〈例〉You need to study more if you want to go to college.

　　　　（あなたはもっと勉強する必要があります、もしあなたが大学に行きたいのなら）

【疑問文】

③If A, 疑問文 B　→　もし A なら、疑問文 B　＊通常 A の後にカンマ（,）を打つ

　　〈例〉If he is free tomorrow, can he come to the game?

　　　　（もし彼に明日時間があるなら、彼は試合に来られますか）

④疑問文 A if B　→　疑問文 A、もし B なら　＊③のように訳される場合もある

　　〈例〉Can he come to the game if he is free tomorrow?

　　　　（彼は試合に来られますか、もし彼に明日時間があるなら）

＋プラス1　**if に続く文では「未来」のことでも現在形を使う**

　if を使って何かを仮定する（条件を言う）場合、未来のことであっても基本的に現在形が使われます。
〈例〉If she is busy tomorrow, she needs to do her homework today.
　　（もし明日彼女が忙しいなら、彼女は宿題を今日する必要があります）

（2）when ＝ 〜の時

【肯定文・否定文】

①When A, B　→　A の時、B　＊通常 A の後にカンマ（,）を打つ

　　〈例〉When I was young, this band was not popular.

　　　　（私が若かった時は、このバンドは人気ではありませんでした）

②A when B　→　A、B の時　＊①のように訳される場合もある

　　〈例〉This band was not popular when I was young.

　　　　（このバンドは人気ではありませんでした、私が若かった時は）

【疑問文】

③When A, 疑問文B　→　Aの時、疑問文B　＊通常Aの後にカンマ（,）を打つ

　　〈例〉When he was using your computer, what were you doing?

　　　　（彼があなたのパソコンを使っていた時、あなたは何をしていたのですか）

④疑問文A when B　→　疑問文A、Bの時　＊③のように訳される場合もある

　　〈例〉What were you doing when he was using your computer?

　　　　（あなたは何をしていたのですか、彼があなたのパソコンを使っていた時）

（3）that ＝ ～ということ、～だと

【肯定文・否定文】

①A that B　→　BということをA

　　〈例〉She was glad that her family was safe.

　　　　（彼女は、彼女の家族が無事で安心しました）

【疑問文】

②疑問文A that B　→　Bということを疑問文A

　　〈例〉Was she glad that her family was safe?

　　　　（彼女は、彼女の家族が無事で安心しましたか）

〈よく使われる A that B〉

　　I know that B　　　＝Bだと私は知っている（私はBだと知っている）

　　I think that B　　　＝Bだと私は思う（私はBだと思う）

　　I hope that B　　　＝Bだと私は望む（私はBだと望む）

　　I remember that B　＝Bだと私は覚えている（私はBだと覚えている）

　　I am sorry that B　＝Bでごめんなさい（ごめんなさい、Bで）

　　I am glad that B　＝Bで私は嬉しく思う（私はBで嬉しく思う）

　　　　　　　　　　　＝Bで私は安心しました（私はBで安心しました）

＋プラス1 「～ということ」のthatは省略可

　「～ということ」という意味のA that B の形では、thatを省略することもできます。

〈例〉I know（that）she is Tom's sister.

　　（私は彼女がトムの妹だと知っています）

全文の和訳を書いていきましょう。またビデオ講義を使って音読の練習も行っていきましょう。

1. Do you want to become a vlogger?

_____

2. What did you want to be when you were little?

_____

3. Did you want to be a professional baseball player? Or did you want to be a doctor?

_____

4. I wanted to be a singer because I liked to sing in front of people.

_____

5. When I was in elementary school, I saw many idols on TV, and I wanted to be like them.

_____

_____

6. I went to karaoke with my sister to practice singing.

_____

7. I joined a dance team to practice dancing, too.

_____

8.	I think I worked very hard, but I noticed that to be a popular singer was really difficult, so I decided to be something else.

_____

_____

9.	But my question was "What do I want to be?"

_____

10.	I liked to write when I was in high school.

_____

11.	In fact, I had a blog website and enjoyed writing articles, so I decided to be a journalist when I grew up.

_____

_____

12.	I studied journalism in college and got a job as a journalist after I graduated.

_____

13.	I am happy to be a journalist because writing articles is fun.

_____

14.	What is my point?

_____

15. I want to say that children's dreams may change when they grow up.

_____

16. Why am I saying this?

_____

17. I am saying this because some surveys done in Japan in 2018 show that many children want to be vloggers when they grow up, and some parents do not think it is a good idea.

_____

_____

_____

18. Who are vloggers?

_____

19. Vloggers are like bloggers, people make money by writing blogs, but vloggers use video.

_____

_____

20. They film themselves and upload their videos on a website to show them to people all over the world.

_____

_____

21. If many people see their videos, they can get money from the website.

_____

22. If you become a popular vlogger, some companies will ask you to advertise their products, so you will be able to get money by using their products in your videos.

_____

_____

23. A YouTuber is another name for a vlogger because many vloggers upload their videos on YouTube, a popular website to share their videos.

_____

_____

24. Some successful vloggers make 100 million yen or more every year.

_____

25. They live in good houses, drive cool cars, and eat good food.

_____

26. It sounds like a great job, but why are some parents against it?

_____

27. They are against it because they think living as vloggers is not easy.

_____

28. They don't think just anyone can do it.

_____

29. In fact, many vloggers cannot make enough money to live.

_____

30. They have a different job because they are not getting any money from the website, so they cannot live just by making their own videos.

_____

_____

31. Some people say that becoming a successful vlogger is like becoming a successful actor because vloggers may have to live poorly until they become famous.

_____

_____

32. You need to be creative, too, because you need to make interesting, funny, or unique videos, so people will want to see your videos.

_____

_____

33. If your videos are not good, nobody will see them, and that means your videos will not make any money.

_____

_____

34. In addition, vloggers need to film themselves, edit their videos, and upload them by themselves, and they need to do this every day!

_____

_____

35. In fact, many famous vloggers in Japan upload 400 or more videos every year.

_____

36. That means they make one or more videos every day.

_____

37. They do not have summer or winter vacations.

_____

38. They must work hard when people are taking a break.

_____

39. It is going to be very difficult if their work is not fun.

_____

40. Some children think that working as a vlogger sounds really good because they can work freely and have fun all the time.

_____

_____

41. Is that true? The answer is "No."

_____

42. Children should know working as a vlogger is hard, but children cannot see that from vloggers' videos, so some parents are worried about that.

_____

_____

43. However, it is not a big problem because children will understand the difficulties when they grow up.

_____

_____

44. In fact, some other surveys done in Japan show that many high schools students think that becoming a vlogger is not realistic.

_____

_____

45. Many high school students answered that they wanted to become teachers, computer programmers, or engineers instead.

_____

_____

46. I am not saying that becoming a vlogger is a bad idea, but it is a unique job.

_____

47.   If you like filming yourself, editing videos and showing them to the world, I think becoming a vlogger is a great idea.

_____

_____

48.   If one of my friends tells me that he or she wants to be a vlogger, I will say go for it because some vloggers are very successful and rich, and he or she may become one of them.

_____

_____

_____

49.   If my daughter tells me she wants to be a vlogger, I will tell her to answer my questions first.

_____

_____

50.   "Are you really sure that you will be able to do this? You may be very poor.

_____

51.   You may not have any vacations, either. Do you really think you will be OK?"

_____

52.   If she answers "Yes" to these questions, I think I will support her.

_____

語句の確認

anyone / anybody	【代】(肯定文)誰でも / (否定文)誰も / (疑問文)誰か
journalist	【名(可算)】ジャーナリスト
author	【名(可算)】著者 / 作家
difficulty	【名(可算)】困難なこと / 難点 【名(不可算)】難しさ / 困難
journalism	【名(不可算)】ジャーナリズム
film	【動】撮影する
upload	【動】アップロードする
mean	【動】意味を表す / 意味する
successful	【形】成功した / 上出来の
own	【形】自分自身の / 自分の

*¹else	【形】その他の / 他の
*²other(＋複数名詞)	【形】他の / 別の
instead	【副】その代わりとして / それよりも
*³however	【副】しかしながら / けれども
against	【前】〜に反対して
as	【前】〜として / 〜だと
in fact	【熟】実際 / はっきり言えば
*⁴all over ○○	【熟】○○のいたるところ
in addition	【熟】さらに / 他に / 加えるに
by *⁵○○ self (複数：○○ selves)	【熟】○○自身で / ○○だけで / ○○1人で

*¹ 基本的に something や anyone などの後に置いて使われる。
　〈例〉Does anyone else want to try it?　(誰か他に挑戦してみたい人はいますか?)
*² 単数名詞を修飾する際は、another が使われる。
　〈例〉I need another desk.　(私はもう1台机が必要です)
　　　　We want to go to other stores.　(私たちは他のお店に行きたいです)
*³ 基本的に文頭や文尾にコンマとともに用いる。多少堅い表現。
　〈例〉I was tired. However, I had to finish this.
　　　　(私は疲れていました。しかしながら私はこれを終わらせないといけませんでした)
*⁴ ○○には、the world や the country などが入る。
　〈例〉He is famous all over the world.　(彼は世界的に有名です)
*⁵ ○○ self や○○ selves の○○の部分には代名詞が入り、「○○自身」という意味になる。

単数	myself(私自身) / yourself(あなた自身) / himself(彼自身) / herself(彼女自身) / itself(それ自身)
複数	ourselves(私たち自身) / yourselves(あなたたち自身) / themselves(彼ら / 彼女ら / それら自身)

まとめを書こう

文の真ん中に足される副詞

フミヤ（Fumiya）とレイチェル（Rachel）の学校での
やりとりの様子を読んで、後の問いに答えましょう。

"Why are you still in the classroom, Fumiya?" Rachel asked him from behind. Fumiya was surprised because he thought he was the only one in the classroom. "Wow. Why did you do that? (　a　) my chair," Fumiya asked. "Oh, I'm sorry. I thought it was funny, but maybe it wasn't. Sorry. (　b　) that again," she answered with a smile, so Fumiya knew she didn't really mean it. "So, what are you doing? Are you doing your homework?" she asked. "No. (　c　) with that. (　d　) a book," Fumiya answered. "What kind of book is it?" asked Rachel. "Oh, gosh. Here we go again. What should I tell her this time?" Fumiya thought. He knew she was going to ask that question because (　e　). When they were watching a Japanese drama together, Fumiya had to translate every single conversation in the drama because she wanted to know everything. He cannot say "I don't want to," because when they met the first time, he told her "I will always help you if you need anything," but he kind of regrets it now.

Rachel is a student from New Zealand and came to Fumiya's high school two weeks ago. Actually, her mother is Japanese, and she is living with her grandparents now. How is her Japanese? Her Japanese language skills are still low because she was born and grew up in New Zealand, so her first language is English. In addition, her mother can speak English very well, so Rachel never had to learn Japanese when she was in New Zealand. However, she always wanted to go to Japan and learn about their culture because she was interested in her background. She was also interested in studying abroad because one of her teachers often said "I never regret studying abroad," so she decided to stay in Japan for a year and go to high school there. She took some classes to practice reading and writing Japanese. She also practiced speaking and listening to Japanese with her mother. They often talked about Rachael's grandparents in Japan because she was planning to live with them.

Rachel likes Fumiya because he is very kind to her. She was surprised at his English when they first met because his English was very good. Why can he speak English so well? He can speak English well because he lived in Canada for two years when he was in elementary school. Rachel sometimes misses speaking English, so she really enjoys talking with him. Does Fumiya like talking with Rachel, too? Yes, he does. He likes it because he can practice speaking English with her. However, he does not want to speak English with her every day because she usually asks many questions, so he gets really tired.

"Oh, this book? This book is about the Japanese economy. Our economy is not very good now. In fact, many people are poor because they cannot find jobs, so I want to know why. Is New Zealand's economy good?" Fumiya asked. "I think it is OK. It is not very good, but I don't think it is terrible, either," Rachel replied. "But I am not a professional (1)economist, so I am not really sure. If you are interested in the economy of New Zealand, you should check out this website," Rachel (2)pulled out her smartphone. "Here. I always use this website to read news from New Zealand. Oh, you should also check out this website. It is very convenient because you can actually watch their news programs." Fumiya looked into the screen and asked "What is the name of the website?" "Oh, it is NZ Reports. I think you can find it pretty easily," Rachel answered. "Alright. I will take a look at it. Thanks," Fumiya took out a notebook and (3)wrote the name. "You are welcome. Do you always stay in the classroom after school?" asked Rachel. "Well, not always, but sometimes because I like to read in a quiet place and our classroom is a perfect place for (4)that," he looked out the window and continued. "I also like (5)the view from here. There aren't any tall buildings, so you can clearly see the sunset from here if the weather is nice. I think it is pretty rare in Tokyo. The leaves change colors, so it is especially beautiful during this season." Rachel also looked out the window. "Do you think we can see the sunset today?" she asked. "I think so. It is almost 4 o'clock, so if you can wait for another 30 minutes, I think you will be able to see it." Rachel looked at her watch and checked the time. She didn't want to miss her bus because her grandparents will worry about her if she is late. She checked her watch again. "I think I have enough time," she thought. "OK. I will wait. I hope it will be good," Rachel said. "Trust me. It will be great!" Fumiya replied.

問題

Q1. (a) 〜 (e) に入る適切な表現をそれぞれ1つずつ選びましょう。

    (a) 1. I almost fell off   2. I fell almost off   3. I off almost fell

    (b) 1. I never will do   2. I will do never   3. I will never do

    (c) 1. I am done already   2. I am already done   3. I already am done

    (d) 1. I was reading actually   2. I was actually reading   3. I actually was reading

    (e) 1. she is always curious   2. she always is curious   3. she is curious always

Q2. 次のうちレイチェルの説明として<u>間違っているもの</u>を1つ選びましょう。

    1. レイチェルの第一言語は英語。

    2. レイチェルはニュージーランドにいた時から日本に行きたいと思っていた。

    3. レイチェルは幼い時から日本語を学んでいた。

    4. レイチェルのお母さんは日本人。

Q3. Rachel moved to Japan. Who does she live with?

_____

Q4. Fumiya's English is good. Why?

_____

Q5. 下線部 (1) の economist の意味は何か次の中から1つ選びましょう。

    1. 環境保護団体   2. 環境に関する研究者   3. 飛行機のエコノミー席   4. 経済学者

Q6. 下線部 (2) で pulled out her smartphone と書かれていますが、その理由を1つ選びましょう。

    1. フミヤとメールアドレスを交換するため。

    2. ニュースが見られるウェブサイトを紹介するため。

    3. フミヤが読んでいる本を検索するため。

    4. 日本の経済状況を調べるため。

Q7. 下線部 (3) に wrote the name と書かれていますが、具体的に何と書いたか英語で答えましょう。

_____

Q8. 下線部 (4) の that が具体的に指す内容を次の中から1つ選びましょう。
1. 静かなところで本を読むこと
2. ニュージーランドのニュースを見ること
3. 英語の勉強をすること
4. 学校の周りの風景を眺めること

Q9. フミヤが好きだと言う下線部 (5) の the view を最も的確に表しているのは、次のうちどれでしょう。

1.

2.

3.

4.

Q10. 次のうち本文の内容とは異なるものを1つ選びましょう。
1. レイチェルは、まだ日本語を上手に話せない。
2. フミヤはレイチェルと毎日英語で話したいとは思っていない。
3. フミヤは日本の経済に興味がある。
4. レイチェルは関西地方に住んでいる。

もうすでに学んだfastやwellといった副詞は、文の後半に足されることが多かったのですが、今回は「be動詞の後」や「一般動詞の前」といった文の真ん中に入る副詞について学んでいきます。基本的には「頻度を表す副詞」と「lyのつく副詞」は、文の真ん中に入れることができます。逆に言えば、fastやwellといった副詞は文の真ん中に入れることができないので注意しましょう。

1. 文の真ん中に足される副詞

副詞	意味	例文
also	～も / また / そのうえ	He can **also** play the piano. （彼はピアノも弾けます / 彼もピアノが弾けます）
almost	ほとんど / もう少しで	She **almost** hit me. （彼女はあと少しで私をたたくところでした）
still	まだ / それでも（なお）	You **still** need to finish this. （あなたはそれでもこれを終わらせる必要があります）
already	もうすでに	I am **already** 25 years old. （私はすでに25歳です）
always	いつも / いつでも	She **always** calls me. （彼女はいつも私に電話します）
usually	いつもは / たいてい	We **usually** go home at six. （私たちはたいてい6時に家に帰ります）
often	しばしば / たびたび	They are **often** late for class. （彼らはしばしば授業に遅刻します）
sometimes	ときどき	I **sometimes** drink coffee. （私は時々コーヒーを飲みます）
*never	決して～ない	He **never** gets tired. （彼は決して疲れません）

＊ never は、すでに否定の意味が含まれているので、肯定文の形で用いられる。
〈例〉He never gets tired. （彼は決して疲れません）　（He never doesn't get tired. ＝ ×）

＋プラス1　副詞の頻度の違いについて

今回登場する副詞の頻度は以下のようになります。

always	＞	usually	＞	often	＞	sometimes	＞	never
（いつも）		（たいてい）		（しばしば）		（ときどき）		（決して～ない）

2.「頻度を表す副詞」や「lyのつく副詞」は、文の真ん中に入れることができる

(1) be動詞の文（進行形、be going toを含む）：be動詞の後に副詞

【肯定文】　主語 ＋ be動詞 ＋ 副詞 ＋ 〜.

　　　　　〈例〉She is **actually** 15 years old. （彼女は実は15歳です）

【否定文】　主語 ＋ be動詞 ＋ not ＋ 副詞 ＋ 〜.

　　　　　〈例〉I am not **usually** tired. （私はいつもは疲れていないです）

【疑問文】　be動詞 ＋ 主語 ＋ 副詞 ＋ 〜?

　　　　　〈例〉Was she **also** playing the piano? （彼女もピアノを弾いていたのですか）

(2) 一般動詞の文：一般動詞の前に副詞

【肯定文】　主語 ＋ 副詞 ＋ 一般動詞 ＋ 〜.

　　　　　〈例〉She **quickly** read the article. （彼女は素早く記事を読みました）

【否定文】　主語 ＋ do / does / did ＋ not ＋ 副詞 ＋ 一般動詞 ＋ 〜.

　　　　　〈例〉He doesn't **usually** sit here. （彼は、いつもはここに座らないです）

【疑問文】　Do / Does / Did ＋ 主語 ＋ 副詞 ＋ 一般動詞 ＋ 〜?

　　　　　〈例〉Do you **still** need this? （あなたはまだこれが必要なのですか）

(3) 助動詞の文：助動詞の後に副詞

【肯定文】　主語 ＋ 助動詞 ＋ 副詞 ＋ 動詞の原形 ＋ 〜.

　　　　　〈例〉You should **also** bring the textbook.

　　　　　　　　（あなたは教科書も持ってくるべきです）

【否定文】　主語 ＋ 助動詞 ＋ not ＋ 副詞 ＋ 動詞の原形 ＋ 〜.

　　　　　〈例〉He will not **always** be there.

　　　　　　　　（彼は、そこにいつもいるわけではないでしょう）

【疑問文】　助動詞 ＋ 主語 ＋ 副詞 ＋ 動詞の原形 ＋ 〜?

　　　　　〈例〉Can you **still** come to the party?

　　　　　　　　（あなたは、それでもパーティーに来られますか）

＋プラス1　__not always ＝ 「いつも〜というわけではない」（部分否定）__

　alwaysが否定文で使われる場合は「いつも〜しない」ではなく「いつも〜するわけではない」という部分否定の形になります。

〈例〉I am not always late. （私はいつも遅れるわけではありません）

　　　　　　　　　　　（私はいつも遅れないです ＝ ×）

文の真ん中で使う副詞の中には「否定文では使われない」「使われ方が変わる」副詞があります。例えば、alsoは否定文ではあまり使われません。またsometimesは、主語の後に置かれることがあります。これらには、あまり理屈がないため、暗記するのがベストだと思います。

〈例〉私は先生でもありません。

I am not also a doctor. ＝ ×　　I am not a doctor, either. ＝ ○

私は時々朝食を食べません。

I don't sometimes eat breakfast. ＝ ×　　I sometimes don't eat breakfast. ＝ ○

全文の和訳を書いていきましょう。またビデオ講義を使って音読の練習も行っていきましょう。

1.　"Why are you still in the classroom, Fumiya?" Rachel asked him from behind.

_____

2.　Fumiya was surprised because he thought he was the only one in the classroom.

_____

3.　"Wow. Why did you do that? I almost fell off my chair," Fumiya asked.

_____

4.　"Oh, I'm sorry. I thought it was funny, but maybe it wasn't. Sorry.

_____

5. I will never do that again," she answered with a smile, so Fumiya knew she didn't really mean it.

_____

_____

6. "So, what are you doing? Are you doing your homework?" she asked.

_____

7. "No. I am already done with that. I was actually reading a book," Fumiya answered.

_____

8. "What kind of book is it?" asked Rachel.

_____

9. "Oh, gosh. Here we go again. What should I tell her this time?" Fumiya thought.

_____

10. He knew she was going to ask that question because she is always curious.

_____

11. When they were watching a Japanese drama together, Fumiya had to translate every single conversation in the drama because she wanted to know everything.

_____

_____

12. He cannot say "I don't want to," because when they met the first time, he told her "I will always help you if you need anything," but he kind of regrets it now.

_____

_____

13. Rachel is a student from New Zealand and came to Fumiya's high school two weeks ago.

_____

_____

14. Actually, her mother is Japanese, and she is living with her grandparents now.

_____

15. How is her Japanese?

_____

16. Her Japanese language skills are still low because she was born and grew up in New Zealand, so her first language is English.

_____

_____

17. In addition, her mother can speak English very well, so Rachel never had to learn Japanese when she was in New Zealand.

_____

_____

18. However, she always wanted to go to Japan and learn about their culture because she was interested in her background.

_____

_____

19. She was also interested in studying abroad because one of her teachers often said "I never regret studying abroad," so she decided to stay in Japan for a year and go to high school there.

_____

_____

_____

20. She took some classes to practice reading and writing Japanese.

_____

21. She also practiced speaking and listening to Japanese with her mother.

_____

22. They often talked about Rachael's grandparents in Japan because she was planning to live with them.

_____

23. Rachel likes Fumiya because he is very kind to her.

_____

24. She was surprised at his English when they first met because his English was very good.

_____

25. Why can he speak English so well?

_____

26. He can speak English well because he lived in Canada for two years when he was in elementary school.

_____

_____

27. Rachel sometimes misses speaking English, so she really enjoys talking with him.

_____

28. Does Fumiya like talking with Rachel, too? Yes, he does.

_____

29. He likes it because he can practice speaking English with her.

_____

30. However, he does not want to speak English with her every day because she usually asks many questions, so he gets really tired.

_____

_____

31.   "Oh, this book? This book is about the Japanese economy.

_____

32.   Our economy is not very good now.

_____

33.   In fact, many people are poor because they cannot find jobs, so I want to know why.

_____

34.   Is New Zealand's economy good?" Fumiya asked.

_____

35.   "I think it is OK.

_____

36.   It is not very good, but I don't think it is terrible, either," Rachel replied.

_____

37.   "But I am not a professional economist, so I am not really sure.

_____

38.   If you are interested in the economy of New Zealand, you should check out this website," Rachel pulled out her smartphone.

_____

_____

39. "Here. I always use this website to read news from New Zealand.

_____

40. Oh, you should also check out this website.

_____

41. It is very convenient because you can actually watch their news programs."

_____

42. Fumiya looked into the screen and asked "What is the name of the website?"

_____

43. "Oh, it is NZ Reports. I think you can find it pretty easily," Rachel answered.

_____

44. "Alright. I will take a look at it. Thanks," Fumiya took out a notebook and wrote the name.

_____

_____

45. "You are welcome. Do you always stay in the classroom after school?" asked Rachel.

_____

46. "Well, not always, but sometimes because I like to read in a quiet place and our classroom is a perfect place for that," he looked out the window and continued.

_____

_____

47. "I also like the view from here.

_____

48. There aren't any tall buildings, so you can clearly see the sunset from here if the weather is nice.

_____

_____

49. I think it is pretty rare in Tokyo.

_____

50. The leaves change colors, so it is especially beautiful during this season."

_____

51. Rachel also looked out the window.

_____

52. "Do you think we can see the sunset today?" she asked.

_____

53. "I think so. It is almost 4 o'clock, so if you can wait for another 30 minutes, I think you will be able to see it."

_____

_____

54. Rachel looked at her watch and checked the time.

_____

55. She didn't want to miss her bus because her grandparents will worry about her if she is late.

_____

_____

56. She checked her watch again. "I think I have enough time," she thought.

_____

57. "OK. I will wait. I hope it will be good," Rachel said.

_____

58. "Trust me. It will be great!" Fumiya replied.

_____

語句の確認

drama	【名(可算)】ドラマ/劇/演劇
conversation	【名(不可算・具体的には可算)】会話/談話/対話
background	【名(不可算)】背景/生い立ち
mistake	【名(不可算・具体的には可算)】間違い/ミス/誤解
view	【名(可算)】景色/眺め 【動】見る/眺める
trust	【名(不可算)】信頼/信用 【動】信用する/信頼する
translate	【動】翻訳する
regret	【動】後悔する/悔いる
single	【形】たった1つ(1人/1個)の
terrible	【形】ひどい/すごく下手/つらい/恐ろしい

professional	【形】専門的な/職業上の
convenient	【形】便利な/使いやすい
perfect	【形】完全な/申し分のない
*1behind	【副】後ろに/後ろを
especially	【副】特に/とりわけ/特別に
abroad	【副】国外へ(に)/海外へ(に)
*2actually	【副】実際に(は)/現に
be surprised (at)	【熟】(～に)驚く
Here we go again.	【熟】ああまたか/ほら始まったぞ
*3kind of～	【熟】～の種類 【熟】(口語)どちらかと言えば～/だいたい～/少し～
*4check out	【熟】調べる/確かめる/(ホテルから)チェックアウトする

*1 behindは副詞だが、here / thereのように、fromを足し「後ろから」という意味として使うこともできる。
　〈例〉Someone called me from behind. （誰かが後ろから私を呼びました）
*2 文頭にActually, と置くことで「実は、」という意味にもなる。
　〈例〉When will you do that? — Actually, I'm doing it right now.
　　（いつ、あなたはそれをする予定ですか。―実は、ちょうど今やっています）
*3 kind ofはくっつけてkindaと発音されることがよくある。
　〈例〉It is kinda cold. （少し寒いですね）
*4 check outはcheck ＋ 目的語 ＋ outの形で使われることもある（目的語が代名詞の時はこの形になる）。
　〈例〉This website is cool. You should check it out. （このサイトは良いです。確認してみるべきです）

まとめを書こう

英語の文型

読んでみよう

大学生のカオリ（Kaori）と彼女の友だちのヘンリー（Henry）のやりとりを読み、後の問題に答えていきましょう。

(Kaori's talking with Henry on the Internet)

Kaori: Hi, Henry. What's going on?

Henry: Hey, Kaori. Doing alright. I'm a little tired, but it's not a problem.

Kaori: Why are you tired?

Henry: Because I had to work today, and I just got off. Working for three hours without taking a break was really tough.

Kaori: Oh, I didn't know you had a part-time job. What do you do?

Henry: I work as a *tutor. I had to teach three children today.

Kaori: How often do you work?

Henry: I work almost every day because I need to pay my (1)college expenses.

Kaori: I see. I hear many college students in America have to work part-time because they usually pay their own college expenses, such as their *tuition and textbooks.

Henry: Right. In addition, I live alone, so I have to pay my living expenses, too. And guess what? It is not unusual.

Kaori: Wow. It is different from many college students in Japan because they don't usually pay their own college expenses.

Henry: Who does then?

Kaori: Their parents do. In addition, if they live away from their family, their parents often pay their living expenses and give them some *allowance, so many students do not need to work at all.

Henry: They are lucky because they don't have to worry about money. In America, some people work full-time for a few years before they start going to college because they think they will not be able to study and work part-time at the same time.

Kaori: That is interesting. How many students do you teach?

Henry: I teach (　　ア　　) students.

Kaori: Wow! You teach many students. (2)<u>No wonder you are busy</u>.

Henry: Right. I teach three elementary school students, one junior high school student, and two high school students. It is tough, but I enjoy teaching them because they are very good students. Some students write me letters, and I really enjoy reading them. (3)<u>(always / happy / me / I / they / make)</u> even when I am in a bad mood. One of my students is only 7 years old, and she calls me Henhen because she cannot say Henry. She is very cute.

Kaori: I see. What do you teach them?

Henry: I teach them many subjects. For example, Math, Science, Social Studies, and English.

Kaori: You teach English, too?

Henry: Oh, I forgot to tell you. Most of my students are Japanese. They came to America because of their fathers' work. Some of them can only speak a little English, so I teach them English. I can speak a little Japanese, so we usually talk in Japanese. I'm glad I took some Japanese classes at college.

Kaori: I see.

Henry: Oh, by the way, one of my American students says he wants to go to college in Japan, so I teach him Japanese. Actually, we are planning to visit Japan this summer. (4)<u>Do you think you can show us around?</u>

Kaori: Well, I live in Tochigi, so if you are going to stay in the Kanto area, I think I can.

Henry: We are planning to visit many places like Miyagi, Tokyo, and Kyoto, so I don't think we are going to stay in the Kanto area. Oh, I know. We are planning to go to *Nikko Toshogu Shrine, so we can see you when we visit there.

Kaori: That sounds good. I grew up in Nikko, so I'll show you some good places around that area. When will you come to Japan?

Henry: We are planning to visit in July. I'll send you the schedule later.

Kaori: OK. I have to tell you something. I will have my final exams in the last week of July, so I won't be able to see you if you will come to Tochigi in that week or the week before.

Henry: I got it.

Kaori: How long will you stay in Japan?

Henry: I think we will only stay for a few days because we don't have much money. We are going to *hitchhike because we don't want to spend much money on transportation.

Kaori: Good idea. I think it will be pretty expensive if you use trains and buses, but I heard night buses were not that bad. Some travelers use night buses because you will be able to sleep on the bus, so you don't have to worry about paying for a hotel. You should check the Internet and find some information.

Henry: OK. I will do that.

Kaori: Oh, one more thing. I have some friends in Tokyo, and they can speak English. Some of them may be able to help you, so I will ask them. But to tell you the truth, I don't think you will need any help in Tokyo if you have a cell phone because you can always use your cell phone if you need to find something, and you will see English signs everywhere, so just don't forget to bring your cell phone *charger.

Henry: Hahaha. OK. I'll remember that.

---

* tutor 家庭教師　　tuition 授業料　　allowance 仕送り/おこづかい　　Nikko Toshogu Shrine 日光東照宮
hitchhike ヒッチハイク（する）　　charger 充電器

問　題

Questions

Q1.　下線部（1）の college expenses の意味は次のうちどれか、1つ選びましょう。

　　1. 大学のキャンパス

　　2. 大学生活でかかる費用

　　3. 高額な時給

　　4. 大学で出会う仲間

Q2. カオリによると、多くの日本の大学生の学費は誰が払っているか日本語で答えましょう。

_____

Q3. 文脈から推測し（ア）に当てはまる英単語を1つ書きましょう。

_____

Q4. 下線部（2）のNo wonder you are busy.の意味に最も近いのは次のうちどれでしょう。
1. そんなに忙しくないでしょう。
2. だからバスを使うのですね。
3. バスを使わないと無理だね。
4. 忙しいわけだ。

Q5. 下線部（3）の（ ）内の語を並べ替えて「（それらは）いつも僕を幸せな気持ちにしてくれます」という文を作りましょう。ただし、不要な単語が1語含まれていますので注意してください。文頭で使う語句の頭文字も小文字表記にしています。

_____

Q6. 次のうち、ヘンリーについて間違っているものを1つ選びましょう。
1. たくさんの生徒を教えている。
2. 一人暮らしをしている。
3. 教えている生徒はみな日本人である。
4. 数学や社会科を教えている。

Q7. 下線部（4）のyou can show us aroundの意味に最も近いのは次のうちどれでしょう。
1. 近くに私たちがいるのが見えますか。
2. 私たちにも見せてくれると思いますか。
3. 私たちのために周りを見ることができますか。
4. 案内してもらうことは可能ですか。

Q8. カオリは、7月の下旬に何かがあるため忙しいです。何があるか、本文から抜き出しましょう。

_____

Q9. カオリは、ヘンリーたちの東京観光は何も問題ないだろうと思っています。その理由はなぜか、日本語で答えましょう。

_____

_____

Q10. 次のうち本文には書かれていないものを1つ選びましょう。

1. ヘンリーたちは、日本に到着したらまず日光東照宮に行く予定である。

2. アメリカでは、学費を稼ぐため大学に入学する前に働く人もいる。

3. カオリには、東京に住んでいる友だちがいる。

4. ヘンリーは、アルバイトを楽しんで行っている。

英語には基本5文型と呼ばれるものがあります。文型とは、簡単に言うと「文の形」。文型を学ぶことで、文章を正しく理解することができるようになります。第1～3文型は、もうすでに練習で何回も登場している形なのですが、第4文型と第5文型は、今回初めて登場する形となります。

1. 文型の説明に使われる4つの基本的要素 (S, V, O, C)

(1) S (Subject)【主語】

・日本語では「～は」「～が」と主に訳される部分。

・主に主語になるのは以下の2つ。

　(a) 名詞（ここでは「冠詞」「所有格」「形容詞」などが名詞につく場合も含める）

　(b) 代名詞

〈例〉**She** likes Japan. （**彼女は**日本が好きです）〈S = She〉

　　　My dog is big. （**私の犬は**大きいです）〈S = My dog〉

(2) V (Verb)【動詞】

・日本語では「～です」「～します」と主に訳される部分。

・主に動詞となるのは以下の3つ。

（a）be動詞

（b）一般動詞

（c）動詞のフレーズ（「be動詞 ＋ 一般動詞ing」「助動詞 ＋ 動詞」など）

〈例〉He **is** a doctor.　（彼は医者**です**）〈V ＝ is〉

I **eat** this every morning.　（私は毎朝これを**食べます**）〈V ＝ eat〉

(3) O（Object）【目的語】

・動詞が表す動作などの対象となる語。

・主に一般動詞の文に登場する（基本的にbe動詞の文には登場しない）。

・主に目的語になるのは以下の2つ。

（a）名詞（ここでは「冠詞」「所有格」「形容詞」などが名詞につく場合も含める）

（b）代名詞

〈例〉She bought **a new camera**.

（彼女は**新しいカメラ**を買いました）〈O ＝ a new camera〉

〈「買ったのは何か？→新しいカメラ」とa new cameraはboughtの対象となっている〉

(4) C（Complement）【補語】

・主語や目的語が「どういうものなのか？」「どういう状態なのか？」を説明する語。

・「be動詞の文」やbecome / lookなどの「主語の様子を表す動詞の文」に登場する。

・主に補語となるのは以下の3つ。

（a）名詞（ここでは「冠詞」「所有格」「形容詞」などが名詞につく場合も含める）

（b）代名詞

（c）形容詞

〈例〉He is **a math teacher**.　（彼は**数学の先生**です）〈C ＝ a math teacher〉

〈「彼はどういう人なのか？→数学の先生」とa math teacherがheを説明している〉

You look **tired**.　（あなたは**疲れて**見えます）〈C ＝ tired〉

〈「あなたはどういう状態なのか？→疲れている」とtiredがyouの状態を説明している〉

＋プラス1　**副詞や副詞句は修飾語のM（Modifier）となる。**

例えば、I study English every day.という文。このevery dayの部分は、S / V / O / Cの何にあたるのかと言いますと…実はどれにも当てはまらず、修飾語のM（Modifier）となります。修飾語には「動詞を説明する副詞」「（時間や場所を表す）前置詞の入っているフレーズ」などがあります。修飾語のMは、S / V / O / Cのように基本的な要素ではないのですが、英語の文ではよく登場しますのでぜひ覚えておきましょう！

〈例〉We finished this **at six**.　（私たちはこれを**6時**に終えました）〈M ＝ at six〉

2. 英語の基本5文型

(1) 第1文型 〈S + V〉

・「主語 + 動詞」の形。SVと呼ばれる。

・多くの場合、SVだけで文が終わるのではなく「動詞を説明する副詞」「(時間や場所を表す) 前置詞が入るフレーズ」などの修飾語が足される。

〈例〉 <u>My brother</u> <u>runs</u> every morning. (私の兄は毎朝走ります)
　　　　　S　　　　　V

(2) 第2文型 〈S + V + C〉

・「主語 + 動詞 + 補語」の形。SVCと呼ばれる。

・S is Cの関係が成り立つ。

・主にSVCで用いられる動詞：be動詞 / become / stay / look / feel / smellなど

〈例〉 <u>The story</u> <u>was</u> <u>very interesting</u>. (お話はとても興味深かったです)
　　　　　S　　　V　　　　C

　　　 <u>You</u> <u>look</u> <u>tired</u>. (あなたは疲れているように見えます)
　　　　S　　V　　C

(3) 第3文型 〈S + V + O〉

・「主語 + 動詞 + 目的語」の形。SVOと呼ばれる。

・多くの場合、Vは一般動詞となり、その動詞が表す動作などの対象となるのがO。

〈例〉 <u>My brother</u> <u>likes</u> <u>Japan</u>. (私の弟は日本が好きです)
　　　　　S　　　　V　　O　　　〈好きなのは何か？→日本〉

(4) 第4文型 〈S + V + O_1 + O_2〉

・「主語 + 動詞 + 目的語 + 目的語」の形。SVOOと呼ばれる。

・基本的な意味は「SがO_1にO_2をVする」。「SVO_2 to O_1」や「SVO_2 for O_1」と同じ意味になる場合がある。

・主にO_1には「人」が入り、O_2には「もの (物・情報など)」が入る。O_2がO_1に移動すること (「もの」が「人」に移動すること) を表す。

・主にSVOOで用いられる動詞：give / teach / buy / show / tell / sendなど

〈例〉 <u>He</u> <u>gave</u> <u>me</u> <u>this apple</u>. (彼は私にこのリンゴをくれました)
　　　　S　V　O_1　O_2　　〈He gave this apple to me.と同じ意味〉

(5) 第5文型 〈S + V + O + C〉

・「主語 + 動詞 + 目的語 + 補語」の形。SVOCと呼ばれる。

・基本的な意味は「SはOをCにVする」。

・Vによって「O is C」の関係が成り立つ。

・主にSVOCで用いられる動詞：make / call / keep / leave / paint など

〈例〉 <u>The news</u> <u>made</u> <u>Hiroshi</u> <u>sad.</u>　（ニュースはヒロシを悲しくさせました）
　　　　S　　　V　　　O　　C　　　　　　　　〈Hiroshi is sad.の関係が成立している〉

＋プラス1　「第4文型〈SVOO〉」と「第5文型〈SVOC〉」の見分け方

（1）He made her a chair.　　　（2）He made her happy.

　第4文型と第5文型を見分けるには、「O（her）」と「最後の単語 / フレーズ（a chair と happy）」との関係を確認する必要があります。「O is 最後の単語 / フレーズ」の関係が成立していれば、第5文型。成立していない場合は、第4文型となります。

　（1）は「She is a chair. ＝ ×」なので、第4文型。つまり、「彼は彼女に椅子を作った」という意味の文になります。（2）は「She is happy. ＝ ○」なので、第5文型。つまり、「彼は彼女を喜ばせた」という意味の文になります。

全文の和訳を書いていきましょう。またビデオ講義を使って音読の練習も行っていきましょう。

(Kaori's talking with Henry on the Internet)
(カオリがインターネットでヘンリーと話している)

1.　*Kaori*:　　Hi, Henry. What's going on?

　　カオリ：＿＿＿＿＿＿＿＿＿＿＿＿＿＿＿＿＿＿＿＿＿＿＿＿＿＿＿＿＿

2.　*Henry*:　　Hey, Kaori. Doing alright. I'm a little tired, but it's not a problem.

　　ヘンリー：＿＿＿＿＿＿＿＿＿＿＿＿＿＿＿＿＿＿＿＿＿＿＿＿＿＿＿＿

3.　*Kaori*:　　Why are you tired?

　　カオリ：＿＿＿＿＿＿＿＿＿＿＿＿＿＿＿＿＿＿＿＿＿＿＿＿＿＿＿＿＿

4. *Henry*: Because I had to work today, and I just got off.

   ヘンリー: _____

5. Working for three hours without taking a break was really tough.

   _____

6. *Kaori*: Oh, I didn't know you had a part-time job. What do you do?

   カオリ: _____

7. *Henry*: I work as a tutor. I had to teach three children today.

   ヘンリー: _____

8. *Kaori*: How often do you work?

   カオリ: _____

9. *Henry*: I work almost every day because I need to pay my college expenses.

   ヘンリー: _____

10. *Kaori*: I see. I hear many college students in America have to work part-time because they usually pay their own college expenses, such as their tuition and textbooks.

    カオリ: _____

    _____

    _____

11. *Henry*: Right. In addition, I live alone, so I have to pay my living expenses, too.

ヘンリー: _____

12. And guess what? It is not unusual.

_____

13. *Kaori*: Wow. It is different from many college students in Japan because they don't usually pay their own college expenses.

カオリ: _____

_____

14. *Henry*: Who does then?

ヘンリー: _____

15. *Kaori*: Their parents do.

カオリ: _____

16. In addition, if they live away from their family, their parents often pay their living expenses and give them some allowance, so many students do not need to work at all.

_____

_____

_____

17. *Henry*: They are lucky because they don't have to worry about money.

ヘンリー: _____

18.   In America, some people work full-time for a few years before they start going to college because they think they will not be able to study and work part-time at the same time.

_____

_____

_____

19.   *Kaori*:   That is interesting. How many students do you teach?

      カオリ: _____

20.   *Henry*:   I teach six students.

      ヘンリー: _____

21.   *Kaori*:   Wow! You teach many students. No wonder you are busy.

      カオリ: _____

22.   *Henry*:   Right. I teach three elementary school students, one junior high school student, and two high school students.

      ヘンリー: _____

_____

23.   It is tough, but I enjoy teaching them because they are very good students.

_____

24.   Some students write me letters, and I really enjoy reading them.

_____

25. They always make me happy even when I am in a bad mood.

_____

26. One of my students is only 7 years old, and she calls me Henhen because she cannot say Henry.

_____

_____

27. She is very cute.

_____

28. *Kaori*: I see. What do you teach them?

カオリ: _____

29. *Henry*: I teach them many subjects.

ヘンリー: _____

30. For example, Math, Science, Social Studies, and English.

_____

31. *Kaori*: You teach English, too?

カオリ: _____

32. *Henry*: Oh, I forgot to tell you. Most of my students are Japanese.

ヘンリー: _____

33.   They came to America because of their fathers' work.

_____

34.   Some of them can only speak a little English, so I teach them English.

_____

35.   I can speak a little Japanese, so we usually talk in Japanese.

_____

36.   I'm glad I took some Japanese classes at college.

_____

37.   *Kaori*:   I see.

      カオリ： _____

38.   *Henry*:   Oh, by the way, one of my American students says he wants to go to college in Japan, so I teach him Japanese.

      ヘンリー： _____

_____

39.   Actually, we are planning to visit Japan this summer.

_____

40.   Do you think you can show us around?

_____

41. *Kaori*: Well, I live in Tochigi, so if you are going to stay in the Kanto area, I think I can.

カオリ: _____

_____

42. *Henry*: We are planning to visit many places like Miyagi, Tokyo, and Kyoto, so I don't think we are going to stay in the Kanto area.

ヘンリー: _____

_____

43. Oh, I know.

_____

44. We are planning to go to Nikko Toshogu Shrine, so we can see you when we visit there.

_____

_____

45. *Kaori*: That sounds good.

カオリ: _____

46. I grew up in Nikko, so I'll show you some good places around that area.

_____

47. When will you come to Japan?

_____

48. *Henry*: We are planning to visit in July. I'll send you the schedule later.

ヘンリー: _____

49. *Kaori*: OK. I have to tell you something.

カオリ: _____

50. I will have my final exams in the last week of July, so I won't be able to see you if you will come to Tochigi in that week or the week before.

_____

_____

51. *Henry*: I got it.

ヘンリー: _____

52. *Kaori*: How long will you stay in Japan?

カオリ: _____

53. *Henry*: I think we will only stay for a few days because we don't have much money.

ヘンリー: _____

_____

54. We are going to hitchhike because we don't want to spend much money on transportation.

_____

_____

55.　*Kaori*:　　Good idea.

　　　カオリ：　_____

56.　　　　　　I think it will be pretty expensive if you use trains and buses, but I heard night buses were not that bad.

　　　　　　_____

　　　　　　_____

57.　　　　　　Some travelers use night buses because you will be able to sleep on the bus, so you don't have to worry about paying for a hotel.

　　　　　　_____

　　　　　　_____

58.　　　　　　You should check the Internet and find some information.

　　　　　　_____

59.　*Henry*:　　OK. I will do that.

　　　ヘンリー：　_____

60.　*Kaori*:　　Oh, one more thing. I have some friends in Tokyo, and they can speak English.

　　　カオリ：　_____

　　　　　　_____

61.　　　　　　Some of them may be able to help you, so I will ask them.

　　　　　　_____

62.   But to tell you the truth, I don't think you will need any help in Tokyo if you have a cell phone because you can always use your cell phone if you need to find something, and you will see English signs everywhere, so just don't forget to bring your cell phone charger.

_____

_____

_____

_____

63.   *Henry*:   Hahaha. OK. I'll remember that.

ヘンリー：_____

語句の確認 Vocabulary

*¹mood	【名(可算)】(その時の)気分/機嫌	part-time	【形】パートタイムの【副】パートタイムで
*²expense	【名(不可算)】出費	full-time	【形】正社員の/常勤の【副】正社員として
transportation	【名(不可算)】乗り物/交通(輸送)機関/輸送	even	【副】～でさえ(も)
pay	【動】(お金を)支払う	everywhere	【副】どこでも
spend	【動】(お金を)使う/費やす/(時を)過ごす	get off	【熟】(列車などから)降りる/仕事が終わる
tough	【形】タフな/困難な	*³one of ○○(複数形名詞)	【熟】○○の1つ
unusual	【形】普通ではない/珍しい	*⁴most (some) of ○○	【熟】○○のほとんどは(いくつかは)
cute	【形】(子ども・商品などが)かわいい	no wonder＋文	【熟】「文」であることが不思議ではない

*1 「良い（悪い）気分でいる」 ＝ be in a good（bad）mood
*2 基本的に「不可算名詞」だが、修飾語を伴ったり「〜用の経費」という意味で使う場合は、可算名詞となる。
　〈例〉college expenses　（大学のための出費）
*3 「複数形名詞」には、them / us といった代名詞が入ることもある。また、「複数形名詞」の前に the や所有格がつくことが多い。
　「〜の1つ」なので3人称単数扱いになるので注意。
　〈例〉One of them is my brother.　（彼らのうちの1人は私の兄です）
　　　 One of my students likes English.　（私の生徒の1人は英語が好きです）
*4 most（some）of 〇〇は、「『特定されている〇〇』のうちのほとんど（いくつか）」という意味なので、基本的に〇〇には the や
　these / those や所有格がつく（the / these / those や所有格が入らない、一般論などを言う場合は of が入らない）。
　〈例〉Most cars are fast.　（〈一般論として〉ほとんどの車は速いです）
　　　 Most of their cars are fast.　（彼らの所有する車のほとんどは速いです）

	可算 / 不可算	単語	例
「少しの〜しかない」 （「ない」という表現）	可算名詞	few	I have **few** pencils.　（私は**数本の**鉛筆**しか**持っていません） *「ほとんど鉛筆を持っていない」といったニュアンス
	不可算名詞	little	I have **little** water.　（私は**少しの**水**しか**持っていません） *「水がこれだけでは足りない」といったニュアンス
「少し〜ある」 （「ある」という表現）	可算名詞	a few	I have **a few** pencils.　（私は**数本**鉛筆を持っています） 「数本持っている」といったニュアンス
	不可算名詞	a little	I have **a little** water.　（私は**少しの**量の水を持っています） 「少しはある」といったニュアンス

* ネイティブによっては「少しの〜しかない」と言う場合は、few / little の代わりに only a few / only a little を使う人もいる。　〈例〉
　I have only a few pencils. / I have only a little water.

まとめを書こう

Review

比較級

ウィルソン先生（Mr. Wilson）による高校の生物学（Biology）の初日の授業が始まろうとしています。説明文を読み、後の問題に答えていきましょう。

Welcome to Biology. I am Ben Wilson, and I will be your teacher. You are in Classroom 209. We have three Biology teachers, and we all teach in different classrooms, so it may be a little confusing. I hope you are in the right place. If you are not, raise your hand. Only one student? Who is your teacher? Ms. Conner? Oh, her class is more difficult than my class. You should stay here. (Students laugh.) Just kidding. Your classroom is 219, so go into the hallway, turn right, and the fourth room on your left will be your classroom. Anyone else? OK. Good. Now I think everybody is in the right place.

OK. It is the first day of class, so let me introduce myself first. I grew up in a small town in California. I think it was smaller than this city, but it was beautiful and had a lot of nature. We had a big lake. Tappan Lake is pretty popular in this area, right? Our lake (a   ) Tappan Lake, but I think it was (b   ). Some people in my hometown may say it is better than Tappan Lake. When I was a little boy, I loved to go there and catch insects. When I was in high school, my favorite subject was Biology. I thought it was easier than other Science classes. In fact, my final grade in Biology was better than my final grades in Chemistry or Physics, so I decided to study Biology in college. When I was in college, I took many Biology classes. They were more interesting than my Biology class in high school, but they were more difficult. I studied really hard, but my grades weren't that good. I didn't fail any classes, but I was close in some classes. It took five years for me to graduate from college, but I was lucky because I got this job right after I graduated.

I have a twin sister and a younger brother. My sister is much smarter than me. We entered the same college at the same time. I don't think she was studying harder than I was, but it took only three and a half years for her to graduate. She is also working as a teacher, but she is teaching Spanish. My brother was a good basketball player when he was in college. He is much taller than I am, so some people don't believe he is my younger brother. What is he doing now? He is working as a basketball coach in our hometown.

Okay, that's enough about me. Now let's talk about this class. I will pass out the (1)syllabus, so you can see my email address, the goals of this class, the class schedule, and so on. I will explain this, but I don't want to make you bored, so I will try to finish it in 10 minutes. First, do you see an email address at the upper right corner? That is my email address. Please contact me anytime. Next, let's talk about the goals of this class…, but let me ask you a question first. If you know the answer, please raise your hand. Ready? (2)What is Biology? What will we learn in this class? Does anyone know the answer? Nobody? That's fine. I think everybody is just shy. I will tell you the answer. Biology is the study of life. It sounds simple, but it is not. Let me give you an example. (3)Please take a look at these two pictures.

Which one is a real duck? Raise your hand if you think the left duck is a real duck? Please raise your hand higher so I can see. OK. All students think this one is a real duck. How about the duck on the right? Do you think it is a real duck? Raise your hand…. Higher, please. OK. Nobody. Well, you are right. The left one is a real duck, but the right one is not, but I have another question. How did you know? What are the differences? Can anyone answer? …. Good. I'm glad nobody can because if you can, you don't have to take this class.

So, the meaning of the word "life" is very difficult to understand. But don't worry, because we are going to talk about it in class, and guess what? Understanding the meaning of the word "life" is one of the main goals of this class. Does it sound difficult? Well, I have to tell you. Some other science classes are much more difficult than Biology.

Oh, no. We are running out of time. OK. I want to explain one more thing before (4)you go, so I will talk more quickly. It is about your schedule. It is on the back of your syllabus. We will have the first experiment next week, so please bring an apron. If you don't have one, go to Super Mart and get one. They have cheap aprons. (5)I think their aprons are cheaper than their potato chips. Okay, that's all for today. I'll see you tomorrow.

問 題

Q1. 次のうち、ウィルソン先生の説明とは異なっているものを1つ選びましょう。

1. 生物学の先生は3人いる。

2. 全ての生物学の授業は、209で行われている。

3. 生物学の担当教員の1人はコナー先生である。

4. ウィルソン先生はカリフォルニアで育った。

Q2. (a) と (b) に入る適切な表現をそれぞれ1つずつ選びましょう。

(a) 1. was not more bigger than　　2. was not more big than　　3. was not bigger than

(b) 1. more beautiful　　　　　　　2. beautifuler　　　　　　　3. beautiful than

Q3. ウィルソン先生が大学で生物学を学ぼうと思った理由を日本語で2つ書きましょう。

1. _____

2. _____

Q4. ウィルソン先生とウィルソン先生のお姉さん（妹さん）は同じ時に大学に入学しましたが、お姉さん（妹さん）の方が早く卒業しました。どれくらい早く卒業したか、日本語で書きましょう。

_____

Q5. 下線部（1）のsyllabusの説明として、最も近いものは次のうちどれでしょう。

1. この日の授業内容が書かれてある紙。

2. 授業初日に行うアンケート。

3. 授業の最初に行う10分程度でできるアクティビティー（課題）。

4. 教員の連絡先や授業の予定など授業概要が書かれている紙。

Q6. 下線部（2）の質問がされた後の状況を一番的確に表しているのは、次のうちどれでしょう。

1.

2.

3.

4.

Q7. ウィルソン先生が、下線部（3）で2つの写真を見せた理由はどれか、次の中から1つ選びましょう。

1. アヒルにはいろいろな種類がいることを見せるため。

2. どちらのアヒルが好みか、生徒に答えさせるため。

3. 「命があるもの」と「命がないもの」の違いを生徒に答えさせるため。

4. 泳いでいる時のアヒルの足は見えないことを伝えるため。

Q8. 下線部（4）のyou goを言い換えるとしたら、次のうち最も適切なのはどれでしょう。

1. you go to the next class.　　　2. you check your syllabus.

3. you take other science classes.　　4. you go running.

Q9. 下線部 (5) を以下の形に言い換える場合、それぞれの（ ）に入る適切な単語は何でしょう。

I think their potato chips are （　　　　　） （　　　　　） （　　　　　） their

aprons.

Q10. 次のうち、本文の内容に合うものを1つ選びましょう。
   1. Mr. Wilson teaches Chemistry.
   2. Students can buy cheap aprons at Super Mart.
   3. Students can find their class schedule on the front of their syllabus.
   4. Students will have their first experiment tomorrow.

　　　　比較級とは「○○より△△」（例えば「私より賢い」「彼より足が速い」など）のように、何かと何かを比較する時に使う表現方法です。基本的な形は"形容詞er ＋ than ＋ 比べるもの"または"副詞er ＋ than ＋ 比べるもの"となります。比べるものが明白な場合は「than ＋ 比べるもの」が省略されます。

1. 比較級は、文の「形容詞」「副詞」の位置に入れるもの

　比較級は一般的な「形容詞」や「副詞」のように使われるため、比較級が入ることで文の種類（be動詞の文、一般動詞の文など）が変わるというものではありません。そのため「肯定文・否定文・疑問文を作る方法」や「文の途中に副詞を足す方法」は、文の種類のルールがそのまま使われます。

〈例〉 He is smart. （be動詞の文）を「コウタより賢い」とする場合。
   【肯定文】 He is smarter than Kota. （彼はコウタより賢いです）
   【否定文】 He is not smarter than Kota. （彼は、コウタより賢くはないです）
   【疑問文】 Is he smarter than Kota? （彼はコウタより賢いのですか）
   【＋副詞】 He is also smarter than Kota. （彼もコウタより賢いです）

> **＋プラス1**　「はるかに」「ずっと」のように比較を強調する場合のmuchとfar
>
> 「彼はコウタよりもはるかに（ずっと）賢いです」と言いたい場合はHe is much (far) smarter than Kota.というように、veryではなくmuchやfarが使われますので注意してください。
> 〈例〉彼は、ベンよりも速く走れます。→He can run faster than Ben.
> 　　　彼は、ベンよりもはるかに速く走れます。→He can run much (far) faster than Ben.
> 　　　　　　　　　　　　　　　　　　（He can run very faster than Ben. ＝ ×）

2. 語尾にerを足すだけでは比較級にできない形容詞や副詞

語尾にerを足すだけでは比較級にできない形容詞や副詞は、いくつかのパターンに分けることができます。

〈普通にはerを足せない形〉

	特徴	例	比較級の形	語尾の変化
パターン1	語尾がe	large	larger	最後に r を足す
パターン2	語尾が〈子音＋y〉	early	earlier	最後のy→iにしてerを足す
パターン3	語尾が〈*短母音＋子音〉	big	bigger	最後の子音を重ねてer

* 短母音とは、短く発音される母音。例えば、bigのiやgetのeの音。カタカナで表すと「ア」「イ」など1文字の音になる。一方で長母音は、長く発音される母音。例えば、seatのea（カタカナだと「イー」）の音やhopeのou（カタカナだと「オウ」）の音。

〈moreを前に足して語尾にerは足さない形〉

	特徴	例	比較級の形
パターン1	つづりが長い形容詞・副詞	important	more important
パターン2	*語尾がlyの副詞	quickly	more quickly

* earlyは除く。

3. good / well / bad / badlyの比較級は、全く違う単語になるので注意

good / well / bad / badlyといった形容詞や副詞の比較級は、全く違う単語になります。

〈不規則な変化をする形容詞・副詞〉

形容詞・副詞	比較級	例文
good〈形容詞〉 （良い）	better （より良い）	His idea is better than mine. （彼のアイデアは私のより良いです）
well〈副詞〉 （上手に）	better （より上手に）	She could sing better than Rin. （彼女はリンより上手に歌えました）
bad〈形容詞〉 （悪い・ひどい）	worse （より悪い・よりひどい）	My car is worse than yours. （私の車はあなたの車よりひどいです）
badly〈副詞〉 （ひどく）	worse （よりひどく）	He drew worse than Zack. （彼はザックよりひどく描きました）

4. 比べるものに代名詞が登場する際は、比べる2つの形をそろえる

比較級の場合、比べるものに代名詞が登場する際は、形（主語 + be動詞、主語 + 一般動詞など）をそろえる必要があります。

例えば「彼女は私よりも若いです」という文は、She is younger than I am. となります。これは、主語のshe がshe isと「主語 + be動詞」の形なので、比べるI もI am と「主語 + be動詞」の形にする必要があるからです（ただし、than の後のbe動詞は省略できます）。

〈例〉彼女は私よりも若いです

She is younger than I am.　　　= ○

She is younger than I.　= ○　（ただし「不自然」だと思うネイティブも多い）

She is younger than me. = △　（会話ではよく使われるが文法上は△）

She is younger than I do.　　　= ×

> ＊ 代名詞以外も比べる2つをそろえる必要があるのですが、多くの場合、be動詞、do / does / did、助動詞は省略した形になっています。
> 〈例〉He is smarter than Bob (is).　　　　She studies harder than Yumi (does).
> 　　　I can run faster than Rin (can).

＋プラス1　比べる2つのものが「何」と「何」なのかに注意！

例えば「私の家はジムの家よりも大きいです」という比較級の文では、比べているのは「私の家」と「ジムの家」です。これが「私の家」と「ジム」にならないように注意する必要があります。

My house is bigger than Jim's house. = ○　（比べるもの：「私の家」と「ジムの家」）
My house is bigger than Jim's. = ○　（比べるもの：「私の家」と「ジムのもの（所有代名詞）」）
My house is bigger than Jim. = ×　（比べるもの：「私の家」と「ジム（本人）」）

しかし、2つのものが異なる場合もあります。例えば「彼女が勉強するよりも私は熱心に勉強しないといけません」という比較級の文は、I must study harder than she does. となります。

これをshe mustに変えてしまうと、「彼女が勉強しないといけないよりも私は熱心に勉強しないといけません（彼女も熱心に勉強しないといけないが、私の方が熱心に勉強しないといけない）」となってしまいます。そのため、ポイントは「何と何を比べているのかをはっきりさせる」というところです。

〈例〉I must study harder than she does.　（私は彼女よりも熱心に勉強しないといけません）
　　　（比べるもの：「私が勉強しないといけない量」と「彼女が日頃から勉強している量」）

全文の和訳を書いていきましょう。またビデオ講義を使って音読の練習も行っていきましょう。

1. Welcome to Biology. I am Ben Wilson, and I will be your teacher.

_____

2. You are in Classroom 209.

_____

3. We have three Biology teachers, and we all teach in different classrooms, so it may be a little confusing.

_____

_____

4. I hope you are in the right place. If you are not, raise your hand.

_____

5. Only one student? Who is your teacher? Ms. Conner?

_____

6. Oh, her class is more difficult than my class. You should stay here. (Students laugh.)

_____

7. Just kidding.

_____

8.   Your classroom is 219, so go into the hallway, turn right, and the fourth room on your left will be your classroom.

_____

_____

9.   Anyone else? OK. Good. Now I think everybody is in the right place.

_____

10. OK. It is the first day of class, so let me introduce myself first.

_____

11. I grew up in a small town in California.

_____

12. I think it was smaller than this city, but it was beautiful and had a lot of nature.

_____

13. We had a big lake. Tappan Lake is pretty popular in this area, right?

_____

14. Our lake was not bigger than Tappan Lake, but I think it was more beautiful.

_____

15. Some people in my hometown may say it is better than Tappan Lake.

_____

16. When I was a little boy, I loved to go there and catch insects.

_____

17. When I was in high school, my favorite subject was Biology.

_____

18. I thought it was easier than other Science classes.

_____

19. In fact, my final grade in Biology was better than my final grades in Chemistry or Physics, so I decided to study Biology in college.

_____

_____

20. When I was in college, I took many Biology classes.

_____

21. They were more interesting than my Biology class in high school, but they were more difficult.

_____

_____

22. I studied really hard, but my grades weren't that good.

_____

23. I didn't fail any classes, but I was close in some classes.

_____

24. It took five years for me to graduate from college, but I was lucky because I got this job right after I graduated.

_____

_____

25. I have a twin sister and a younger brother. My sister is much smarter than me.

_____

26. We entered the same college at the same time.

_____

27. I don't think she was studying harder than I was, but it took only three and a half years for her to graduate.

_____

_____

28. She is also working as a teacher, but she is teaching Spanish.

_____

29. My brother was a good basketball player when he was in college.

_____

30. He is much taller than I am, so some people don't believe he is my younger brother.

31. What is he doing now? He is working as a basketball coach in our hometown.

32. Okay, that's enough about me. Now let's talk about this class.

33. I will pass out the syllabus, so you can see my email address, the goals of this class, the class schedule, and so on.

34. I will explain this, but I don't want to make you bored, so I will try to finish it in 10 minutes.

35. First, do you see an email address at the upper right corner? That is my email address.

36. Please contact me anytime.

37. Next, let's talk about the goals of this class ..., but let me ask you a question first.

_____

38. If you know the answer, please raise your hand. Ready? What is Biology?

_____

39. What will we learn in this class? Does anyone know the answer? Nobody?

_____

40. That's fine. I think everybody is just shy. I will tell you the answer.

_____

41. Biology is the study of life. It sounds simple, but it is not.

_____

42. Let me give you an example. Please take a look at these two pictures.

_____

43. Which one is a real duck? Raise your hand if you think the left duck is a real duck?

_____

44. Please raise your hand higher so I can see. OK.

_____

45. All students think this one is a real duck. How about the duck on the right?

_____

46. Do you think it is a real duck? Raise your hand.... Higher, please.

_____

47. OK. Nobody. Well, you are right.

_____

48. The left one is a real duck, but the right one is not, but I have another question.

_____

49. How did you know? What are the differences? Can anyone answer? .... Good.

_____

50. I'm glad nobody can because if you can, you don't have to take this class.

_____

51. So, the meaning of the word "life" is very difficult to understand.

_____

52. But don't worry, because we are going to talk about it in class, and guess what?

_____

53. Understanding the meaning of the word "life" is one of the main goals of this class.

_____

54. Does it sound difficult?

_____

55. Well, I have to tell you. Some other science classes are much more difficult than Biology. Oh, no. We are running out of time. OK.

_____

_____

56. I want to explain one more thing before you go, so I will talk more quickly.

_____

57. It is about your schedule. It is on the back of your syllabus.

_____

58. We will have the first experiment next week, so please bring an apron.

_____

59. If you don't have one, go to Super Mart and get one. They have cheap aprons.

_____

60. I think their aprons are cheaper than their potato chips.

_____

61. Okay, that's all for today. I'll see you tomorrow.

_____

語句の確認

insect	【名(可算)】昆虫
syllabus	【名(可算)】授業の概要書 / シラバス
duck	【名(可算)】アヒル / カモ
*1potato chip	【名(可算)】ポテトチップス
experiment	【名(可算)】(科学上の)実験
apron	【名(可算)】エプロン / 前掛け
twin	【名(可算)】双子の1人 【形】双子の
nature	【名(不可算)】自然 / 天然
meaning	【名(不可算・具体的には可算)】意味

fail	【動】失敗する / (試験などに)落ちる / 単位を落とす
raise	【動】(高く)持ちあげる / (手を)あげる / 育てる
confusing	【形】混乱させる(ような)
bored	【形】退屈した
main	【形】主な / 主要な
*2upper	【形】上のほうの / 高いほうの
In fact, ～.	【熟】実際、～。/ もっとはっきり言えば、～。
run out of～	【熟】～がなくなる / ～を使い果たす / ～を切らす
pass out～	【熟】～を配る / ～を配布する

*1 通常potato chipsと複数形で用いられる
*2 反対語はlower ＝ 下のほうの / 低いほうの

まとめを書こう

最上級

Let's Read!
読んでみよう

ジョン（John）が日本についてプレゼンテーションをしています。プレゼンの内容を読み、後の問題に答えていきましょう。

Good morning, everyone. I'm John Collins. Today, I will talk about Japan. Many people think it is a small island country. In fact, it is much smaller than America, but it has more than 6,800 islands. To tell you the truth, it is not a small country in the world. Take a look at (1)this list. It shows the sizes of Asian countries. There are more than 40 countries in the list. Do you think Japan is the smallest country? The answer is "No." The smallest country in Asia is *Maldives. How about Japan? It *rankes 19th, so it is actually larger than many other countries in Asia.

I lived in Kagawa Prefecture for three years when I was little. Where is Kagawa? It is in the Shikoku area, and it is the smallest prefecture in Japan. How about the biggest? Hokkaido is the biggest prefecture of all. It is much bigger than the Kanto area, so it is huge! When I was in Japan, I found many interesting things, so let me talk about them.

First of all, Japan is safe. I think it is one of the safest countries in the world. Many people in big cities work late and go home by train or bus. How about in America? I don't think you can do the same thing. If you work in a downtown area and need to work late all the time, you should go to work by car for your security. (2)Don't get me wrong. Walking outside alone at night is still dangerous in Japan, but only a few people will choose to go to work by car just because they don't want to walk alone in the dark.

And.... This is another example. Please take a look at this picture. (Shows a (3)picture.) Can you believe they have vending machines on the street? It is hard to imagine in our country because it is too dangerous to have vending machines on the street. Why? Because some bad people will try to steal money from them, but it is not true in Japan. People are so nice in this country. If you drop your wallet somewhere, you will have a good chance to find it at the closest police box. It

110

doesn't sound usual for other countries.

Second, Japan is beautiful. Why do I think so? Because most parts of Japan have four seasons, and you can enjoy different things in each season. For example, people can enjoy beautiful flowers during spring. Cherry blossoms bloom during this season, and many people enjoy them with their friends, family, students, and so on. They often bring food and drinks and have a party. This kind of party has a name. It is a (　ア　) party. During this season, if you go to a park with beautiful cherry blossoms on weekends, (4)it is the worst. You may not be able to walk through the park because there are too many people.

What do Japanese people do in summer? They enjoy watching fireworks and going to big summer festivals. Many people wear yukatas (summer kimonos) to those events, so it is pretty interesting. I went to some big festivals when I was in Japan. For example, I went to the Kanto Festival in Akita, the Gion Festival in Kyoto, and the Awa Dance Festival in Tokushima. They were great, but I thought the Awa Dance Festival was the best of the three because I could join the dance. It was very exciting. The dance is not that difficult, so I think anyone can do it. If you are interested, you can watch some videos of the festival on the Internet, so please take a look at them.

Autumn is a colorful season in Japan. Leaves change their colors and look beautiful. Japanese has many mountains. In fact, the mountains cover more than 70% of the land of Japan, so you can enjoy beautiful trees everywhere. I climbed many mountains when I was in Japan, and they were really beautiful. I especially liked Mount Rokko in Hyogo Prefecture. I think it was the best mountain of all. They have a *ropeway, and the view from there is so beautiful. If you get a chance to visit Hyogo during autumn, you should go to Mount Rokko.

Finally, you can see beautiful Christmas lights in winter. Many big parks and department stores *are decorated with beautiful lights, and you can see some of them for free. One of the most popular places to visit during this season is Gotemba Kogen Resort. I went there with my friends a few years ago, and we could see many areas for free, so it was amazing.

So, I think Japan is a great country. You can also enjoy their high-tech toilets, anime, sushi, and so on, so please visit Japan if you have a chance. That's it for my presentation. Thank you.

---

* Maldives モルディブ共和国　　rank 〇〇（順位の）〇〇位に位置する　　ropeway ロープウェイ
be decorated with 〜　〜で装飾されている

問 題 Questions

Q1. 下線部（1）の this list の上位3つを最も適切に表しているのは次のうちどれでしょう。

1.

1.	China	1,370,793,000 people
2.	India	1,309,173,000 people
3.	Indonesia	237,310,000 people

2.

1.	Russia	17,100,000 km²
2.	China	9,600,000 km²
3.	India	3,290,000 km²

3.

1.	Maldives	325,000 people
2.	Brunei	401,890 people
3.	Macau	573,003 people

4.

1.	Russia	17,100,000 km²
2.	Canada	9,980,000 km²
3.	America	9,830,000 km²

Q2. 下線部（2）の don't get me wrong の意味に最も近いものは次のうちどれでしょう。

1. 私は間違っていませんよ。

2. 私は違うものを手に入れてしまいました。

3. 勘違いしないでください。

4. 私の捕まえる時は間違えないでください。

Q3. 下線部（3）の picture は、次のうちどれが最も適切でしょう。

1.

2.

3.

4.

Q4. ジョンが「日本人は優しい」と感じる例を1つあげています。それは何か、日本語で答えましょう。

_____

Q5. （ア）に入る最も適切な単語を1つ選びましょう。
1. Shichigosan　　2. Oshogatsu　　3. Obon　　　4. Hanami

Q6. なぜ、ジョンは下線部（4）の it is the worst. と言ったか、その理由を日本語で答えましょう。

_____

Q7. ジョンが参加した夏のお祭りの中で、一番良いと思ったお祭りは何か<u>英語</u>で答えましょう。

_____

Q8. ジョンによると日本の秋で美しいものは何か次の中から1つ選びましょう。
1. ロープウェイ　　2. 秋空　　　　3. 紅葉　　　　4. 花

Q9. ジョンが、冬の日本で楽しめるものとして、あげているものは何か次の中から1つ選びましょう。
1. クリスマスのイルミネーション
2. 大きな公園でのイベント
3. デパートでの買い物
4. 六甲山でのハイキング

Q10. 次のうち本文の内容とは<u>異なる</u>ものを1つ選びましょう。
1. John lived in Kagawa when he was in Japan.
2. John thinks people never walk in downtown areas in Japan.
3. John thinks going to Gotenba Kogen Resort in winter is a good idea.
4. People in Japan enjoy viewing cherry blossoms during spring.

ここがポイント

最上級とは「家族の中で最も若い」「私たちのクラスの中で一番速く走れる」など「○○の中で一番（最も）△△」と表現したいときに使われる言い方です。基本的な形は"the ＋ 形容詞est"または"(the ＋) 副詞est"となります（副詞の場合は、theを省略することも可）。前回学んだ比較級と似ている箇所もいくつかあります。

1. 比較級同様、最上級も文の「形容詞」「副詞」の位置に入れる

比較級の時と同様、最上級も「形容詞」「副詞」のように使われるため、最上級を入れることによって文の種類（be動詞の文、一般動詞の文など）が変わることはありません。そのため「肯定文・否定文・疑問文を作る方法」や「文の途中に副詞を足す方法」は、比較級と同様に文の種類のルールがそのまま使われます。

〈例〉He can run fast.（助動詞の文）を「クラスで一番速く」とする場合。

【肯定文】 He can run (the) fastest in the class.
（彼はクラスで一番速く走れます）

【否定文】 He cannot run (the) fastest in the class.
（彼は、クラスで一番速く走れません）

【疑問文】 Can he run (the) fastest in the class?
（彼はクラスで一番速く走れるのですか）

【＋副詞】 He can still run (the) fastest in the class.
（彼はまだクラスの中で一番速く走れます）

> **＋プラス1** the ＋ 形容詞est ＋ 名詞の形
>
> 最上級は「一番背が高いです」ではなく「一番背が高い生徒です」のように、形容詞 ＋ 名詞の形でも使うことができます。この場合は「形容詞est」の後に「名詞」を足せば完成となります。
>
> 〈例〉He is the tallest student in his class. （彼はクラスの中で最も背の高い生徒です）
> That is the closest supermarket. （あれが一番近いスーパーです）

2. 最上級の文で使われる in と of

　最上級が使われる文で「～の中で」と範囲を表す際、主に使われるのは in と of です。これらの大きな違いは以下の通りです。

(1) in ○○

　○○には、1つの集団・グループが入る（クラス、国、市町村、世界など）。

〈イメージ〉

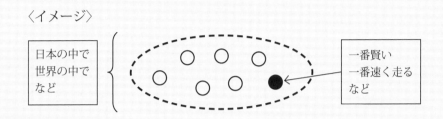

(2) of △△

　△△には、以下の4種類のパターンが入る。

①**all**　（全体の中で / みんなの中で）

〈例〉He is the smartest **of all**.（彼は**みんなの中で**一番賢いです）

②**the 数字**　（○人の中で・○個の中で）

〈例〉He is the tallest **of the five**.（彼は**5人の中で**一番背が高いです）

③**all the 複数名詞**　（すべての複数名詞の中で）

〈例〉He is the fastest **of all the students**.（彼は**全ての生徒の中で**一番足が速いです）

④**us all / them all**　（私たちの中で / 彼らの中で）

〈例〉He studies (the) hardest **of us all**.（彼は**私たちの中で**一番熱心に勉強します）

〈イメージ〉

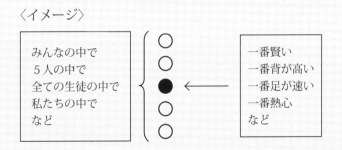

　これらの in ○○ や of △△ は「何の中なのか？（どのグループの中なのか？ / どの人たちの中でなのか？など）」が明白な場合は、省略することも可能です。

3. 語尾にestを足すだけでは最上級にできない形容詞や副詞

　比較級同様、語尾にestを足すだけでは最上級にできない形容詞や副詞は、いくつかのパターンに分けることができます。これらの単語は、基本的に比較級の時に例外とされた単語と同じ単語です。

〈普通にはestを足せない形〉

	特徴	例	最上級	語尾の変化
パターン1	語尾がe	large	largest	最後に st を足す
パターン2	語尾が〈子音＋y〉	early	earliest	最後のy→iにしてestを足す
パターン3	語尾が〈短母音＋子音〉	big	biggest	最後の子音を重ねてest

〈mostを前に足して語尾にestは足さない形〉

	特徴	例	最上級
パターン1	つづりが長い形容詞・副詞	important	most important
パターン2	*語尾がlyの副詞	quickly	most quickly

＊ earlyは除く。

4. good / well / bad / badlyの最上級は、全く違う単語になるので注意。

　こちらも比較級同様、good / well / bad / badlyといった形容詞や副詞の最上級は、全く違う単語になりす。

〈不規則な変化をする形容詞・副詞〉

形容詞・副詞	最上級	例文
good〈形容詞〉 （良い）	best （一番良い）	His idea is the best. （彼のアイデアは一番良いです）
well〈副詞〉 （上手に）	best （一番上手に）	She could sing the best. （彼女が一番上手に歌えました）
bad〈形容詞〉 （悪い・ひどい）	worst （一番悪い・一番ひどい）	My car is the worst of the three. （私の車は、3台の中で最低です）
badly〈副詞〉 （ひどく）	worst （一番ひどく）	I drew the worst in the group. （私はグループで最もひどく描きました）

＋プラス1　よく使われる"one of the 最上級"の形

　英語では「一番○○の1つ」という意味で"one of the 最上級"という形がよく使われます。日本人の感覚からすると「え？　一番なんだから、1つしかないんじゃないの?」となると思うのですが、英語では違うんですね。日本語で言う「（素晴らしいという意味で使われる）最高」という言葉に近いニュアンスだと思います（例えば「あの映画は最高に良かった≠今まで自分が見てきた映画の中で、No.1の映画」のような使い方）。

〈例〉He is one of the smartest students in my class.　（彼はクラスの中で最も賢い生徒の一人です）

全文の和訳を書いていきましょう。またビデオ講義を
使って音読の練習も行っていきましょう。

1. Good morning, everyone. I'm John Collins. Today, I will talk about Japan.

_____

2. Many people think it is a small island country.

_____

3. In fact, it is much smaller than America, but it has more than 6,800 islands.

_____

4. To tell you the truth, it is not a small country in the world.

_____

5. Take a look at this list. It shows the sizes of Asian countries.

_____

6. There are more than 40 countries in the list.

_____

7. Do you think Japan is the smallest country?

_____

8. The answer is "No." The smallest country in Asia is Maldives. How about Japan?

_____

9. It rankes 19th, so it is actually larger than many other countries in Asia.

_____

10. I lived in Kagawa Prefecture for three years when I was little. Where is Kagawa?

_____

11. It is in the Shikoku area, and it is the smallest prefecture in Japan.

_____

12. How about the biggest? Hokkaido is the biggest prefecture of all.

_____

13. It is much bigger than the Kanto area, so it is huge!

_____

14. When I was in Japan, I found many interesting things, so let me talk about them.

_____

15. First of all, Japan is safe. I think it is one of the safest countries in the world.

_____

16. Many people in big cities work late and go home by train or bus.

_____

17. How about in America? I don't think you can do the same thing.

_____

18. If you work in a downtown area and need to work late all the time, you should go to work by car for your security.

_____

_____

19. Don't get me wrong.

_____

20. Walking outside alone at night is still dangerous in Japan, but only a few people will choose to go to work by car just because they don't want to walk alone in the dark.

_____

_____

21. And.... This is another example. Please take a look at this picture.

_____

22. (Shows a picture.) Can you believe they have vending machines on the street?

_____

23. It is hard to imagine in our country because it is too dangerous to have vending machines on the street.

_____

_____

24. Why? Because some bad people will try to steal money from them, but it is not true in Japan.

_____

_____

25. People are so nice in this country.

_____

26. If you drop your wallet somewhere, you will have a good chance to find it at the closest police box.

_____

_____

27. It doesn't sound usual for other countries.

_____

28. Second, Japan is beautiful. Why do I think so?

_____

29. Because most parts of Japan have four seasons, and you can enjoy different things in each season.

_____

_____

30. For example, people can enjoy beautiful flowers during spring.

_____

31. Cherry blossoms bloom during this season, and many people enjoy them with their friends, family, students, and so on.

_____

_____

32. They often bring food and drinks and have a party.

_____

33. This kind of party has a name. It is a Hanami party.

_____

34. During this season, if you go to a park with beautiful cherry blossoms on weekends, it is the worst.

_____

_____

35. You may not be able to walk through the park because there are too many people.

_____

36. What do Japanese people do in summer?

_____

37. They enjoy watching fireworks and going to big summer festivals.

_____

38. Many people wear yukatas (summer kimonos) to those events, so it is pretty interesting. I went to some big festivals when I was in Japan.

_____

_____

39. For example, I went to the Kanto Festival in Akita, the Gion Festival in Kyoto, and the Awa Dance Festival in Tokushima.

_____

_____

40. They were great, but I thought the Awa Dance Festival was the best of the three because I could join the dance.

_____

_____

41. It was very exciting. The dance is not that difficult, so I think anyone can do it.

_____

42. If you are interested, you can watch some videos of the festival on the Internet, so please take a look at them.

_____

_____

43. Autumn is a colorful season in Japan. Leaves change their colors and look beautiful.

_____

44. Japanese has many mountains. In fact, the mountains cover more than 70% of the land of Japan, so you can enjoy beautiful trees everywhere.

_____

_____

45. I climbed many mountains when I was in Japan, and they were really beautiful.

_____

46. I especially liked Mount Rokko in Hyogo Prefecture.

_____

47. I think it was the best mountain of all.

_____

48. They have a ropeway, and the view from there is so beautiful.

_____

49. If you get a chance to visit Hyogo during autumn, you should go to Mount Rokko.

_____

50. Finally, you can see beautiful Christmas lights in winter.

_____

51. Many big parks and department stores are decorated with beautiful lights, and you can see some of them for free.

_____

_____

52. One of the most popular places to visit during this season is Gotemba Kogen Resort.

_____

53. I went there with my friends a few years ago, and we could see many areas for free, so it was amazing.

_____

_____

54. So, I think Japan is a great country. You can also enjoy their high-tech toilets, anime, sushi, and so on, so please visit Japan if you have a chance.

_____

_____

55. That's it for my presentation. Thank you.

_____

語句の確認

Asia	【名(固有)】アジア	land	【名(不可算)】陸/陸地
prefecture	【名(可算)】県 / 府	security	【名(不可算)】セキュリティー /安全/安心
fireworks	【名(可算)】(通常複数形で)花火	spring	【名(不可算)】春
vending machine	【名(可算)】自動販売機	autumn / fall	【名(不可算)】秋
*1cherry blossom	【名(可算)】桜の花	bloom	【動】花が咲く / 開花する
size	【名(可算)】サイズ/大きさ	imagine	【動】想像する
downtown	【名(可算)】都市部/ダウンタウン 【形】都市部の 【副】都市部に	cover	【動】覆う /(分野・研究などを)含む・学習する
		don't get me wrong	【熟】誤解しないでください
		*2First of all, 〜	【熟】第一に、〜

*1 通常 cherry blossoms と複数形で用いられる。

*2 First of all, でなく First, (最初に) とすることも可。また、論点をいくつか並べるのに、Second, (2番目に) や Finally, (最後に) という表現もよく使われる。

まとめを書こう

原級比較の as 〜 as

Let's Read!

読んでみよう

ミツル（Mitsuru）とワカコ（Wakako）のやりとりを読み、後の問題に答えていきましょう。

Mitsuru: It's a beautiful day. I am glad the (1)rainy season is finally over.

Wakako: I know. I don't think it rained as much as last year.

Mitsuru: I hate the rainy season because I often have to take a bus to go to school. If it is sunny or cloudy, I go to school by bicycle. It takes about 40 minutes, so it is a little far, but if I take the back road, there are not as many traffic lights as on the main street, so I can go pretty fast. I can also enjoy the great scenery, so I like going to school by bicycle. But if it is raining, I go to school by bus because then going to school by bicycle is dangerous.

Wakako: I don't like taking a bus to school.

Mitsuru: I don't like it, either. It's terrible because it is always full. The passengers are mainly students and workers, so I think they are using the bus for (2)similar reasons to mine.

Wakako: I see.

Mitsuru: June is the worst month of the year for me because riding a (3)packed bus for about 30 minutes to go to school is not fun at all, and we usually have our final exams in the first week of July, so I have to study for them.

Wakako: Right. Exams. How did they go?

Mitsuru: They went okay. Did you get all of your exams back?

Wakako: Not yet, but I got some of them back. I got 90 on my Math exam and 70 on my Biology exam. My other exam scores were not as good as my Math exam, but they were better than my Biology exam. How about you?

Mitsuru: Mine were not that good because I didn't study as hard as you did. I got 75 on my English exam, but that was my highest. My parents were not

	that happy to see the scores, but it doesn't matter. It is not the end of the world, and the summer break is (4)<u>just around the corner</u>! I can't wait.
Wakako:	That's right. The summer break is going to start in ten days. We will have a lot of homework, but I think we will have enough time to finish it.
Mitsuru:	I know. I like summer because we don't have to go to school, but I don't like days with high temperatures. It is getting hotter and hotter! You might die if you stay outside for too long. I'm not kidding. We had to cancel our soccer game last year because it was too hot.
Wakako:	I know. The weather forecast says it will get worse in August, so let's hope it won't get as bad as last year. Do you have any plans over (5)<u>the break</u>?
Mitsuru:	I am planning to take a computer programming course because I want to make games for smartphones, and we cannot learn much about it in our high school.
Wakako:	I see.
Mitsuru:	We will not have any classes outside, so I don't have to worry about getting a *heat stroke.
Wakako:	Hahaha. That's right. You know what? That sounds interesting. I want to take that course, too. Do you think it is too late?
Mitsuru:	Let me check. I think I have the schedule on my smartphone.... Oh, you are lucky (　　ア　　), so you must *register as soon as you can.
Wakako:	Really? Nice! I will do it right after I get back home. Do I need anything for the course?
Mitsuru:	You need to have your own computer because you won't be able to borrow one.
Wakako:	Oh, no. My computer is really old. I think I bought it 7 years ago. Should I get a new one?
Mitsuru:	I think my computer is as old as yours. It is a little slow, but it is fast enough to write codes, so you don't need to get a new computer.
Wakako:	Sounds good. When will the course start?
Mitsuru:	It will start in the last week of July. The course is only 5 days long, but we will be studying 6 hours every day, so I think we will learn a lot. We will make a simple smartphone game on the last two days, so I am very excited.
Wakako:	What kind of smartphone game do you want to make?

Mitsuru: I want to make a free game to learn English. I think learning English from textbooks is boring, so I want to make a different way to learn English. You can go to an English school after school or on weekends, but it will be expensive, so it is not for everybody. I think every student should have an equal chance to learn English, so I want to make (6)this game.

Wakako: Wow. That's cool.

Mitsuru: Thanks. But I am not really sure if it will be popular because I think learning English will not be as important as learning other subjects.

Wakako: Why not?

Mitsuru: Well, it is because our smartphones are now working as *translators, and they are really good. You can have a regular conversation without any problems, and it is getting better and better, so we may not need to learn English in the near future.

Wakako: That's interesting.

* heat stroke 熱中症　　register 登録する　　translator 翻訳機/翻訳家

問　題

Q1.　下線部（1）rainy season を日本語に訳すと何になるか書きましょう。

_____

Q2.　下線部（2）similar reasons to mine とは具体的にどのような理由か次の中から1つ選びましょう。

1. 自転車だと通学・通勤に40分ほどかかる。
2. 6月が嫌い。
3. 通学にバスを使うのが嫌い。
4. 雨が降っているといつも使っている交通手段が使えない。

Q3.　下線部（3）の packed に近い意味の単語を本文から抜き出しましょう。

_____

Q4.　現在のところ返却された、ワカコとミツルの試験結果で正しいものは次のうちどれか、1つ選びましょう。

1.

ワカコ		ミツル	
現代文	83	古文	72
生物学	70	物理	68
物理	78	英語	75
英語	72	数学	62
数学	90	地理	70
地理	75	日本史	65

2.

ワカコ		ミツル	
現代文	73	古文	72
生物学	70	物理	70
物理	62	英語	75
英語	75	数学	90
数学	68	地理	90
地理	64	日本史	80

3.

ワカコ		ミツル	
現代文	92	古文	72
生物学	70	物理	68
物理	66	英語	75
英語	71	数学	62
数学	90	地理	70
地理	85	日本史	65

4.

ワカコ		ミツル	
現代文	73	古文	77
生物学	70	物理	74
物理	81	英語	75
英語	75	数学	90
数学	90	地理	70
地理	79	日本史	62

Q5. 下線部 (4) のjust around the cornerに最も近い意味のフレーズは次のうちどれでしょう。

1. 宿題も何もない
2. 角を曲がったところ
3. ちょうど角のあたり
4. もうすぐそこ

Q6. 下線部 (5) のthe breakは、何のことを言っているか次の中から1つ選びましょう。

1. 次の休み時間
2. この夏休み
3. この週末
4. パソコンの故障

Q7. (ア) に入る最も適切なフレーズを次の中から1つ選びましょう。

1. because you cannot take this course
2. because you have a good computer
3. because the deadline is tomorrow
4. because you have a smartphone

Q8. ミツルの7月〜8月はじめのスケジュールは次のうちどれでしょう。

1.

July						
Sun	Mon	Tue	Wed	Thu	Fri	Sat
	1 期末試験 ———	2	3	4	5 ⟶	6
7 部活	8	9 部活	10：今日	11 プログラミング 申し込み締め切り	12 部活	13
14	15	16 部活	17	18	19 部活	20 夏休み開始!
21 部活	22	23 部活	24	25	26 部活	27
28	29 プログラミング ———	30	31	8/1	8/2 ⟶	8/3

2.

July						
Sun	Mon	Tue	Wed	Thu	Fri	Sat
	1	2 部活休み	3	4	5 部活休み	6
7 部活休み	8 **期末試験** ⟶	9	10：今日	11	12 部活	13
14 部活	15	16 部活	17 プログラミング 申し込み締め切り	18	19 部活	20 夏休み開始！
21 部活	22	23 部活	24	25	26 部活	27
28	29 プログラミング ⟶	30	31	8/1	8/2	8/3

3.

July						
Sun	Mon	Tue	Wed	Thu	Fri	Sat
	1 **期末試験** ⟶	2	3	4	5	6
7 部活	8	9 部活	10：今日	11 部活	12 プログラミング 申し込み締め切り	13
14 部活	15	16 部活	17	18 部活	19	20 夏休み開始！
21 部活	22 プログラミング ⟶	23	24	25	26	27
28	29 プログラミング ⟶	30	31	8/1	8/2	8/3

4.

July						
Sun	Mon	Tue	Wed	Thu	Fri	Sat
	1 **期末試験** ⟶	2	3	4	5	6
7 部活	8	9 部活	10：今日	11 プログラミング 申し込み締め切り	12 部活	13
14 部活	15	16 部活	17 夏休み開始！	18	19 部活	20
21 部活	22 プログラミング ⟶	23	24	25	26	27
28	29 プログラミング ⟶	30	31	8/1	8/2	8/3

Q9. 下線部 (6) の this game は具体的にどんなゲームか日本語で答えましょう。

_____

Q10. 次のうち本文の内容とは異なるものを1つ選びましょう。

1. ミツルは自転車で通学するのが好き。

2. ワカコは新しいパソコンを買う予定。

3. ミツルの両親はミツルの試験の結果にそんなに満足していなかった。

4. ミツルはスマートフォン用のゲームを作りたいと考えているが人気が出るかは自信がない。

as〜asで「彼女はダイゴと同じぐらい背が高い」「彼は（彼の）お父さんと同じぐらい速く走れる」といった「同じぐらい〜」ということを表すことができます。基本的な形は "as 形容詞 as" や "as 副詞 as" となり、形容詞/副詞は原級（erやestなどをつけない形）が使われるのがポイントです。

1. as〜asは様々な種類の文（be動詞、一般動詞、助動詞など）で使える

　as〜as も比較級/最上級と同様に、文の形容詞/副詞の箇所に使われるため、様々な種類の文で使うことができます。基本的に、文章の形容詞/副詞が使われるところにas〜asのフレーズを入れるだけで完成となります。

【be動詞の文】　　She is tall.　（彼女は背が高いです）
　　　　　　　　　　　　↓
　　　　　　　　She is as tall as Daigo.　（彼女はダイゴと同じぐらい背が高いです）

【一般動詞の文】　I practiced hard.　（私は熱心に練習しました）
　　　　　　　　　　　　↓
　　　　　　　　I practiced as hard as Nanami.
　　　　　　　　（私はナナミと同じぐらい熱心に練習しました）

【助動詞の文】　　He can run fast.　（彼は速く走れます）
　　　　　　　　　　　　↓
　　　　　　　　He can run as fast as his father.
　　　　　　　　（彼は彼のお父さんと同じぐらい速く走れます）

＋プラス1　She is as tall as Daigo. は、She is tall. という意味ではない

　as〜as の文を訳す際は、形容詞や副詞の意味に引っ張られないように注意する必要があります。例えば、She is as tall as Daigo. は「彼女はダイゴと同じぐらい背が高いです」とよく訳されますが、正確には「彼女はダイゴと同じぐらいの背の高さです」といった意味になります。つまり、ダイゴの背が低い場合は、彼女も背が低いということになります。そのため、She is tall. にはならないので注意してください。

　同様に、He can run as fast as his father. も「彼は彼のお父さんと同じぐらい速く走れます」とよく訳されますが、彼のお父さんの足が遅い場合、彼も足が遅いということになります。

2. 否定文、疑問文、副詞の足し方は、文の種類のルールをそのまま使う

比較級/最上級と同様に、否定文、疑問文、副詞の足し方は、文の種類 (be動詞の文、一般動詞の文、助動詞の文など) のルールをそのまま使います。しかし、否定文の訳は「○○と同じぐらい〜ではない」ではなく「○○ほど〜ではない」となるので注意してください。例えば、She is not as tall as Daigo. という文は「彼女はダイゴと同じぐらい背が高くない (＝2人とも背が低い)」ではなく「彼女はダイゴほど背が高くない (＝彼女は背が高いかもしれないがダイゴほどではない)」となります。

〈例〉He can run as fast as John. （彼はジョンと同じぐらい速く走れます）【助動詞の文】

　　【否定文】He <u>cannot</u> run as fast as John. （彼はジョンほど速くは走れません）

　　【疑問文】<u>Can</u> he run as fast as John? （彼はジョンと同じぐらい速く走れるのですか）

　　【＋副詞】He can <u>still</u> run as fast as John. （彼はまだジョンと同じぐらい速く走れます）

3. many / much を使って「同じぐらいの数の/量の○○」「同じ程度」も表すことができる

"as many ○○ as" で「同じぐらいの数の○○ (可算名詞)」、"as much △△ as" で「同じぐらいの量の△△ (不可算名詞)」を表すことができます。また、"as much as" だけで「同じ程度・同じ量」を表すこともできます。

〈例〉Taro has <u>as many pens as</u> Jim.

　　（タロウは、ジムと同じぐらいの本数のペンを持っています。）

　　I need <u>as much water as</u> Mika. （私はミカと同じぐらいの量の水が必要です。）

　　He always eats <u>as much as</u> his brother. （彼はいつも彼のお兄さんと同じ量を食べます。）

＋プラス1　　"as much △△ as" は、"△△ as much as" の形にできないので注意

先ほど登場したI need <u>as much water as</u> Mika. （私はミカと同じぐらいの量の水が必要です）は、I need <u>water as much as</u> Mika. とは、表せないので注意してください。同様にHe always eats as much as his brother. （彼はいつも彼のお兄さんと同じ量を食べます）という文を「同じ量のお米を食べます」に変える場合は、He always eats <u>as much rice as</u> his brother. （He always eats rice as much as his brother. ＝ ×）となるので注意してください。

134

4. 比べるものに代名詞が登場する際は、比べているものに注意（比べる2つの形をそろえる）

　as 〜 asの文も比較級同様、比べるものの形（主語 + be動詞、主語 + 一般動詞など）に注意する必要があります。例えば「彼女は彼と同じぐらい賢いです」という文を作る場合。She is as smart as he is. となります。これは、主語のshe がshe isと「主語 + be動詞」の形なので、比べるものもhe isと「主語 + be動詞」の形にするからです（ただし、2つ目asの後のbe動詞は省略できます）。

〈例〉彼女は彼と同じぐらい賢いです

　　　She is as smart as he is. 　　= ○

　　　She is as smart as he. 　　　= ○（ただし「不自然」と思うネイティブも多い）

　　　She is as smart as him. 　　　= △（会話ではよく使われるが文法上は△）

　　　She is as smart as he does. = ×

> ＊ 代名詞以外も比べる2つをそろえる必要があるのですが、多くの場合、be動詞、do / does / did、助動詞は省略した形になっています。
> 　〈例〉 He is as smart as Bob (is). 　　　　　She studies as hard as Yumi (does).
> 　　　　（彼はボブと同じぐらい賢いです）　　（彼女はユミと同じぐらい熱心に勉強します）
> 　　　　I can run as fast as Rin (can).
> 　　　　（私はリンと同じぐらい速く走れます）

＋プラス1　比べる2つをそろえなくてもいい場合

　実は「意図していることが違う」場合、比べるものをそろえなくても文法上問題ないということがあります。以下の2文のように、意図することが異なる場合、そろえる形が変わってきますので注意しましょう。

　（1）You should study English as hard as he does.
　　　（あなたは彼が勉強する量と同じぐらい勉強するべきです）
　　　= 彼は日頃から勉強している。その量と同じぐらいあなたも勉強するべき。
　（2）You should study English as hard as he should.
　　　（あなたは彼が勉強するべき量と同じぐらい勉強するべきです）
　　　= 彼は勉強するべき。その量と同じぐらいあなたも勉強するべき。

---

5. 覚えておきたいas 〜 asを使ったフレーズ

(1) as 〜 as possible ＝ 可能なかぎり〜、できるかぎり〜

　〈例〉I need it as soon as possible. 　（私はそれが可能な限り早く必要です）

(2) as 〜 as △△ can ＝ △△が可能なかぎり〜、△△ができるかぎり〜

　〈例〉I ran as fast as I could. 　（私は〈私が〉できる限り速く走りました）

全文の和訳を書いていきましょう。またビデオ講義を
使って音読の練習も行っていきましょう。

1. *Mitsuru*: It's a beautiful day. I am glad the rainy season is finally over.

ミツル: _____

2. *Wakako*: I know. I don't think it rained as much as last year.

ワカコ: _____

3. *Mitsuru*: I hate the rainy season because I often have to take a bus to go to school.

ミツル: _____

4.   If it is sunny or cloudy, I go to school by bicycle.

_____

5.   It takes about 40 minutes, so it is a little far, but if I take the back road, there are not as many traffic lights as on the main street, so I can go pretty fast.

_____

_____

_____

6.   I can also enjoy the great scenery, so I like going to school by bicycle.

_____

7. But if it is raining, I go to school by bus because then going to school by bicycle is dangerous.

_____

_____

8. *Wakako*: I don't like taking a bus to school.

ワカコ: _____

9. *Mitsuru*: I don't like it, either. It's terrible because it is always full.

ミツル: _____

10. The passengers are mainly students and workers, so I think they are using the bus for similar reasons to mine.

_____

_____

11. *Wakako*: I see.

ワカコ: _____

12. *Mitsuru*: June is the worst month of the year for me because riding a packed bus for about 30 minutes to go to school is not fun at all, and we usually have our final exams in the first week of July, so I have to study for them.

ミツル: _____

_____

_____

13. *Wakako*: Right. Exams. How did they go?

ワカコ: _____

14. *Mitsuru*: They went okay. Did you get all of your exams back?

ミツル: _____

15. *Wakako*: Not yet, but I got some of them back.

ワカコ: _____

16. I got 90 on my Math exam and 70 on my Biology exam.

_____

17. My other exam scores were not as good as my Math exam, but they were better than my Biology exam. How about you?

_____

_____

18. *Mitsuru*: Mine were not that good because I didn't study as hard as you did.

ミツル: _____

19. I got 75 on my English exam, but that was my highest.

_____

20. My parents were not that happy to see the scores, but it doesn't matter.

_____

21.   It is not the end of the world, and the summer break is just around the corner! I can't wait.

_____

_____

22.   *Wakako*: That's right. The summer break is going to start in ten days.

      ワカコ: _____

23.   We will have a lot of homework, but I think we will have enough time to finish it.

_____

_____

24.   *Mitsuru*: I know. I like summer because we don't have to go to school, but I don't like days with high temperatures.

      ミツル: _____

_____

25.   It is getting hotter and hotter!

_____

26.   You might die if you stay outside for too long. I'm not kidding.

_____

27.   We had to cancel our soccer game last year because it was too hot.

_____

28. *Wakako*: I know. The weather forecast says it will get worse in August, so let's hope it won't get as bad as last year.

ワカコ: _____

29. Do you have any plans over the break?

_____

30. *Mitsuru*: I am planning to take a computer programming course because I want to make games for smartphones, and we cannot learn much about it in our high school.

ミツル: _____

_____

_____

31. *Wakako*: I see.

ワカコ: _____

32. *Mitsuru*: We will not have any classes outside, so I don't have to worry about getting a heat stroke.

ミツル: _____

_____

33. *Wakako*: Hahaha. That's right. You know what? That sounds interesting.

ワカコ: _____

34.   I want to take that course, too. Do you think it is too late?

_____

35.   *Mitsuru*: Let me check. I think I have the schedule on my smartphone....

     ミツル: _____

36.   Oh, you are lucky because the deadline is tomorrow, so you must register as soon as you can.

_____

_____

37.   *Wakako*: Really? Nice! I will do it right after I get back home.

     ワカコ: _____

38.   Do I need anything for the course?

_____

39.   *Mitsuru*: You need to have your own computer because you won't be able to borrow one.

     ミツル: _____

_____

40.   *Wakako*: Oh, no. My computer is really old.

     ワカコ: _____

41.   I think I bought it 7 years ago. Should I get a new one?

_____

42.   *Mitsuru*: I think my computer is as old as yours.

       ミツル: _____

43.   It is a little slow, but it is fast enough to write codes, so you don't need to get a new computer.

_____

_____

44.   *Wakako*: Sounds good. When will the course start?

       ワカコ: _____

45.   *Mitsuru*: It will start in the last week of July.

       ミツル: _____

46.   The course is only 5 days long, but we will be studying 6 hours every day, so I think we will learn a lot.

_____

_____

47.   We will make a simple smartphone game on the last two days, so I am very excited.

_____

_____

48.　*Wakako*:　What kind of smartphone game do you want to make?

　　　ワカコ:　_____

49.　*Mitsuru*:　I want to make a free game to learn English.

　　　ミツル:　_____

50.　　　　　I think learning English from textbooks is boring, so I want to make a different way to learn English.

　　　　　_____

　　　　　_____

51.　　　　　You can go to an English school after school or on weekends, but it will be expensive, so it is not for everybody.

　　　　　_____

　　　　　_____

52.　　　　　I think every student should have an equal chance to learn English, so I want to make this game.

　　　　　_____

　　　　　_____

53.　*Wakako*:　Wow. That's cool.

　　　ワカコ:　_____

54. *Mitsuru*: Thanks. But I am not really sure if it will be popular because I think learning English will not be as important as learning other subjects.

ミツル: _____

_____

55. *Wakako*: Why not?

ワカコ: _____

56. *Mitsuru*: Well, it is because our smartphones are now working as translators, and they are really good.

ミツル: _____

_____

57. You can have a regular conversation without any problems, and it is getting better and better, so we may not need to learn English in the near future.

_____

_____

58. *Wakako*: That's interesting.

ワカコ: _____

語句の確認

rainy season	【名(可算)】梅雨 / 雨季	packed	【形】満員の / いっぱい詰まった
*¹weather forecast	【名(可算)】天気予報	similar（to）	【形】似ている / 類似した
scenery	【名(不可算)】風景 / 景色	terrible	【形】ひどい / 恐ろしい / 厳しい
passenger	【名(可算)】乗客 / 旅客	possible	【形】可能な / 考えられる
exam	【名(可算)】試験	regular	【形】一般的な / 普通の / 規則的な
score	【名(可算)】点数 / 得点	finally	【副】ついに / 最後に / やっと
end	【名(可算)】終わり / 最後【動】終える	○○(形容詞) enough to ～	【熟】～するには十分○○
programming	【名(不可算)】プログラミング	back road	【熟】裏道
code	【名(不可算・具体的には可算)】コード【動】コーディングする	*³You know what?	【熟】ねぇ聞いて / あのさ / ねぇ知っている
*²matter	【動】問題となる / 重要である		

*1 forecastは、「予想【名（可算）】」「予想する【動】」という意味。
*2 よく it doesn't matter (if ～ or not). の形で使われ「(もし～であっても、もしくは～でなくても) 問題ではない」と訳される。
　〈例〉It doesn't matter if they are smart or not. (彼らが賢いか賢くないかは、問題ではない)
*3 You know what? は、Guess what? と同じように使われる。

まとめを書こう

比較級・最上級 応用編

大学生のヒロコ（Hiroko）とエリック（Erick）の会話、その後のジョンソン先生（Prof. Johnson）の説明を読み、後の問題に答えていきましょう。

Erick:	Hey Hiroko, how are you?
Hiroko:	I'm sleepy. I woke up at five and could not sleep after that, so I decided to study a little bit.
Erick:	Wow. That's good.
Hiroko:	Well, my grades were bad last year, so I need to study much harder this year.
Erick:	Really? Which class was the most difficult?
Hiroko:	Chemistry. No doubt. It was (1)a nightmare. I think no other class is more difficult than Chemistry. I am pretty sure I studied more than any other student in my class, but I got a B. I was trying to get an A, but I couldn't.
Erick:	Well, that is not bad. I took Chemistry last year and got a C. I know it is not a good grade, but I could pass the class, so I was glad. Do you think you got the highest score?
Hiroko:	I doubt it. I don't think I got the highest score, but I think I got at least third highest score in my class.
Erick:	That is good. You should be proud of yourself. Which class was the second hardest class?
Hiroko:	Let's see. World History was pretty difficult. I am not good at remembering names of people or places, so my final grade was not that good.
Erick:	What did you get?
Hiroko:	（　ア　）．
Erick:	That's good. I took World History two years ago, and my grade was worse.
Hiroko:	What did you get?

Erick: I got a C. I had to turn in a paper every week, but I didn't have a computer, so I had to do it at the library. It was difficult.

Hiroko: Really? We had to write only three papers throughout the course, so it was not that bad.

Erick: Are you taking any Social Studies classes this year?

Hiroko: Yes. I am taking two, (2)Economics and Asian History.

Erick: Really? How are they? Which is more interesting?

Hiroko: They are good. I think Economics is more interesting. Actually, I have Economics next period.

Erick: Oh, do you have to go now?

Hiroko: No. I need to go to the library before the class, but I still have 40 more minutes, so I'm fine.

Erick: Who do you have for Economics?

Hiroko: I have Prof. Johnson. Why?

Erick: Because I took Economics last year and had Prof. Evans. Some students didn't like his class because of his teaching style.

Hiroko: What do you mean?

Erick: Well, he always gave us a question like "What is money?" "How should we use our money?" and "Why things are so expensive today?" at the beginning of each class. We had to write the answers on a piece of paper and give it to him at the end of class. He usually repeated the answers a few times during class, so it was not that difficult, but (3)a few students were complaining.

Hiroko: I see. I think Prof. Johnson sometimes does the same thing, too, but not all the time. Which class was easier, World History or Economics?

Erick: Economics was. I liked it because I learned many things from that class.

Hiroko: I see. Oh, sorry. I have to go now.

Erick: Alright. See you.

(In Prof. Johnson's Economics class)

Good afternoon, everyone. As I announced last time, we are going to talk about the history of money today. I think most of you have some kind of money in your pocket or your bag right now. We use coins and paper money, but I think it is interesting because they are just pieces of *metal and paper. Think about it. Why do we believe they are so *valuable? Many people work very hard to earn them. Some people try to steal them from other people, and (4)it gets worse sometimes. In other words, money has so much power. Many people try to earn as much money as possible. But why? Was it always like this? Where did the first money come from? When did people make it? Why did people make it? Which type of money did people make first, paper money or coins? We are going to answer these kinds of questions, so let's begin.

As you may know, people used many different things for money before they invented coins and paper money. For example, people in one area used cows and sheep for money. People in another area used *shells, so people did have some kind of money, but they were not the same.

So, where did the first money come from? The answer is... we don't know, but some scientists say people in *Turkey made coins about 3,000 years ago, and they were the oldest type of money. Why did they make coins? Because they needed to pay *tax to the government. That was the main reason, but they soon started using coins to buy things and sell things, too, because coins were much easier to carry around.

How about paper money? Chinese people invented the first paper money about 1,000 years ago, but many people didn't like the idea first. Why? That'll be the first question on (5)this worksheet. When you get one, I want you to start talking with your neighbors and write down your answer. I will give you 10 minutes. If you have questions, let me know. I want you to share your ideas with the class after the discussion, so be ready, OK? Let's begin.

* metal 金属　　valuable 高価な/貴重な　　shell 貝　　Turkey トルコ　　tax 税金

問 題

Q1.　下線部 (1) の a nightmare の意味は何か次の中から1つ選びましょう。
1. 真夜中　　　　2. 徹夜　　　　　　3. 正夢　　　　　4. 悪夢

Q2.　（ア）に入る最も適切な文を次の中から1つ選びましょう。
1. I got a C　　2. I got a B　　3. I got a new camera　　4. I got a new computer

Q3. 下線部 (2) のEconomicsの意味は何か次の中から1つ選びましょう。
1. 政治学　　　　　2. 地理学　　　　　3. 経済学　　　　　4. 法律学

Q4. 下線部 (3) のa few students were complaining と似た意味のフレーズを本文から6語で抜き出しましょう。

_____

Q5. ヒロコはエリックとの会話の後でどこに向かったか次の中から1つ選びましょう。
1. 図書館　　　2. 次の授業の教室　　　3. ジョンソン先生のオフィス　　　4. 食堂

Q6. ジョンソン先生の授業ではこの日何について話したか日本語で答えましょう。

_____

Q7. 下線部 (4) のit gets worse sometimes に含まれるものを次の中から1つ選びましょう。
1. お金のために一生懸命働くこと
2. お金のために人生を台無しにするような重い罪を犯すこと
3. お金のために生きるのが馬鹿らしく感じること
4. お金のためにギャンブルを始めること

Q8. 最初の紙幣は、いつ・どこで誕生したか日本語で答えましょう。

いつ：_____　　　　どこ：_____

Q9. 下線部 (5) のthis worksheet の説明として正しいものを、1つ選びましょう。
1. 前回の授業で配られたものである
2. 授業の最後に提出しないといけない
3. 自分一人で答えを見つけないといけない
4. 10分で最初の問題に答えないといけない

Q10. 次のうち本文には書かれていないものを1つ選びましょう
1. ヒロコは化学の成績がクラスでトップ3には入っていたと思っている
2. エリックが取った世界史の授業は、毎週レポートを書く必要があった
3. エバンズ先生は、世界史を教えている
4. ジョンソン先生によると、最初に作られたお金は硬貨で、のちに紙幣が作られた

今回は比較級を使って最上級を表す方法や、最上級を使って「○○番目に〜」を表す方法を学んでいきます。基本となるのは比較級・最上級の形なので、これらがしっかり身についていないと理解するのが難しいでしょう。

1. which を使った比較級・最上級

「どれが〜」や「どの○○が〜」などを表す which は比較級や最上級でよく使われます。

(1) Which 〜? = どれが〜ですか（主語をたずねる疑問文）

〈例〉I found three supermarkets. —**Which** is the closest?

（私は3つのスーパーを見つけました。—どれが一番近いですか）

(2) Which ○○ 〜? = どの○○が〜ですか（主語をたずねる疑問文）

〈例〉**Which computer** is the most expensive?（どのパソコンが一番高いですか）

(3) Which 〜, ○○ or □□? =「○○と□□では、どちらが〜ですか」

〈例〉**Which** is longer, this movie **or** that movie?

（この映画とあの映画ではどちらの方が長いですか）

2. 比較級応用編

比較級には副詞として使える more than や、最上級を表すことができる形などもあります。

(1) 副詞としての more than 〜 =「〜よりももっと」「〜よりもさらに」

〈例〉She studied English **more than** I did.（彼女は私よりも英語を勉強しました）

(2) 差を具体的に表す方法

○○ + 比較級 than =「○○歳年上、○○倍食べる」など（○○ = 時間、長さ、〜倍）

〈例〉She is **four years older than** I am.（彼女は私よりも4歳年上です）

His room is **three times bigger than** my room.

（彼の部屋は私の部屋の3倍大きいです）

(3) 比較級を使って最上級を表す方法①

No (other) ○○ + 比較級 than 〜 =「〜より…な○○はない」（○○ = 単数形の名詞）

〈例〉**No (other) student** in my class is **smarter than** she is.

= She is the smartest student in my class.

（彼女より賢い生徒は私のクラスにはいません

= 彼女が私のクラスで一番賢い生徒です）

(4) 比較級を使って最上級を表す方法②

比較級 than + any other ○○ =「他のどの○○よりも…」（○○ = 単数形の名詞）

〈例〉I think Hokkaido is **more beautiful than any other prefecture** in Japan.

= I think Hokkaido is the most beautiful prefecture in Japan.

（北海道は日本の他のどの県よりも美しいと思います

= 北海道が日本で一番美しい県だと思います）

3. 最上級応用編・順位を表す方法

最上級は「2番目に賢い」のように「○○番目に～」といったことも表すことができます。

the ＋ 序数 ＋ 最上級 ＝「○○番目に～」（序数 ＝ first, second, third, etc)

〈例〉He is **the second fastest** student in my school.

（彼は私の学校で2番目に速い生徒です）

全文の和訳を書いていきましょう。またビデオ講義を使って音読の練習も行っていきましょう。

1.　*Erick*:　　Hey Hiroko, how are you?

エリック：＿＿＿＿＿＿＿＿＿＿＿＿＿＿＿＿＿＿＿＿＿＿＿＿＿＿＿

2.　*Hiroko*:　I'm sleepy. I woke up at five and could not sleep after that, so I decided to study a little bit.

ヒロコ：＿＿＿＿＿＿＿＿＿＿＿＿＿＿＿＿＿＿＿＿＿＿＿＿＿＿＿

＿＿＿＿＿＿＿＿＿＿＿＿＿＿＿＿＿＿＿＿＿＿＿＿＿＿＿

3.　*Erick*:　　Wow. That's good.

エリック：＿＿＿＿＿＿＿＿＿＿＿＿＿＿＿＿＿＿＿＿＿＿＿＿＿＿＿

4.　*Hiroko*:　Well, my grades were bad last year, so I need to study much harder this year.

ヒロコ：＿＿＿＿＿＿＿＿＿＿＿＿＿＿＿＿＿＿＿＿＿＿＿＿＿＿＿

＿＿＿＿＿＿＿＿＿＿＿＿＿＿＿＿＿＿＿＿＿＿＿＿＿＿＿

5. *Erick*: Really? Which class was the most difficult?

   エリック: _____

6. *Hiroko*: Chemistry. No doubt. It was a nightmare.

   ヒロコ: _____

7.   I think no other class is more difficult than Chemistry.

   _____

8.   I am pretty sure I studied more than any other student in my class, but I got a B.

   _____

   _____

9.   I was trying to get an A, but I couldn't.

   _____

10. *Erick*: Well, that is not bad. I took Chemistry last year and got a C.

    エリック: _____

11.   I know it is not a good grade, but I could pass the class, so I was glad.

    _____

12.   Do you think you got the highest score?

    _____

13. *Hiroko*:　I doubt it. I don't think I got the highest score, but I think I got at least third highest score in my class.

ヒロコ:　_____

_____

14. *Erick*:　That is good. You should be proud of yourself.

エリック:　_____

15.　Which class was the second hardest class?

_____

16. *Hiroko*:　Let's see. World History was pretty difficult.

ヒロコ:　_____

17.　I am not good at remembering names of people or places, so my final grade was not that good.

_____

_____

18. *Erick*:　What did you get?

エリック:　_____

19. *Hiroko*:　I got a B.

ヒロコ:　_____

20. *Erick*: That's good. I took World History two years ago, and my grade was worse.

エリック: _____

21. *Hiroko*: What did you get?

ヒロコ: _____

22. *Erick*: I got a C. I had to turn in a paper every week, but I didn't have a computer, so I had to do it at the library. It was difficult.

エリック: _____

_____

23. *Hiroko*: Really? We had to write only three papers throughout the course, so it was not that bad.

ヒロコ: _____

_____

24. *Erick*: Are you taking any Social Studies classes this year?

エリック: _____

25. *Hiroko*: Yes. I am taking two, Economics and Asian History.

ヒロコ: _____

26. *Erick*: Really? How are they? Which is more interesting?

エリック: _____

27. *Hiroko*: They are good. I think Economics is more interesting.

ヒロコ： _____

28. Actually, I have Economics next period.

_____

29. *Erick*: Oh, do you have to go now?

エリック： _____

30. *Hiroko*: No. I need to go to the library before the class, but I still have 40 more minutes, so I'm fine.

ヒロコ： _____

_____

31. *Erick*: Who do you have for Economics?

エリック： _____

32. *Hiroko*: I have Prof. Johnson. Why?

ヒロコ： _____

33. *Erick*: Because I took Economics last year and had Prof. Evans.

エリック： _____

34. Some students didn't like his class because of his teaching style.

_____

35. *Hiroko*: What do you mean?

ヒロコ: _____

36. *Erick*: Well, he always gave us a question like "What is money?" "How should we use our money?" and "Why things are so expensive today?" at the beginning of each class.

エリック: _____

_____

_____

37. We had to write the answers on a piece of paper and give it to him at the end of class.

_____

_____

38. He usually repeated the answers a few times during class, so it was not that difficult, but a few students were complaining.

_____

_____

39. *Hiroko*: I see. I think Prof. Johnson sometimes does the same thing, too, but not all the time. Which class was easier, World History or Economics?

ヒロコ: _____

_____

40. *Erick*: 　Economics was. I liked it because I learned many things from that class.

　　エリック: _____

41. *Hiroko*: 　I see. Oh, sorry. I have to go now.

　　ヒロコ: 　_____

42. *Erick*: 　Alright. See you.

　　エリック: _____

(In Prof. Johnson's Economics class) (ジョンソン先生の経済学の授業にて)

43. Good afternoon, everyone.

　　_____

44. As I announced last time, we are going to talk about the history of money today.

　　_____

45. I think most of you have some kind of money in your pocket or your bag right now.

　　_____

46. We use coins and paper money, but I think it is interesting because they are just pieces of metal and paper.

　　_____

　　_____

47. Think about it. Why do we believe they are so valuable?

　　_____

48. Many people work very hard to earn them.

_____

49. Some people try to steal them from other people, and it gets worse sometimes.

_____

50. In other words, money has so much power.

_____

51. Many people try to earn as much money as possible. But why?

_____

52. Was it always like this? Where did the first money come from?

_____

53. When did people make it? Why did people make it?

_____

54. Which type of money did people make first, paper money or coins?

_____

55. We are going to answer these kinds of questions, so let's begin.

_____

56. As you may know, people used many different things for money before they invented coins and paper money.

_____

_____

57. For example, people in one area used cows and sheep for money.

_____

58. People in another area used shells, so people did have some kind of money, but they were not the same.

_____

_____

59. So, where did the first money come from?

_____

60. The answer is... we don't know, but some scientists say people in Turkey made coins about 3,000 years ago, and they were the oldest type of money.

_____

_____

61. Why did they make coins? Because they needed to pay tax to the government.

_____

62. That was the main reason, but they soon started using coins to buy things and sell things, too, because coins were much easier to carry around.

_____

_____

63. How about paper money?

_____

64. Chinese people invented the first paper money about 1,000 years ago, but many people didn't like the idea first.

_____

_____

65. Why? That'll be the first question on this worksheet.

_____

66. When you get one, I want you to start talking with your neighbors and write down your answer.

_____

_____

67. I will give you 10 minutes. If you have questions, let me know. I want you to share your ideas with the class after the discussion, so be ready, OK? Let's begin.

_____

_____

語句の確認 Vocabulary

nightmare	【名(可算)】悪夢(の様な出来事)
coin	【名(可算)】硬貨/コイン
government	【名(可算)】政府/内閣 【名(不可算)】政治
paper	【名(不可算)】(素材としての)紙 【名(可算)】(小)論文/レポート
*1doubt	【名(不可算・具体的には可算)】 疑い/疑問 【動】疑う
*2wake	【動】(眠りから)覚める/起こす
mean	【動】意味する/意味を表す
repeat	【動】繰り返す/繰り返し言う
complain	【動】不平を言う/愚痴をこぼす

announce	【動】発表する/アナウンスする
earn	【動】(働いて)稼ぐ/儲ける
invent	【動】発明する/考え出す
own	【形】自分自身の/自分の
proud (of〜)	【形】(〜を)誇りに思って
throughout	【前】〜を通してずっと
as 〜	【接】〜した通り/〜のように
*3the year before	【熟】その前の年
*4a piece of 〜	【熟】1枚の〜/1つの〜/1個の
so far	【熟】ここまで/これまで
turn in 〜	【熟】(〜を)提出する
In other words, 〜	【熟】言い換えれば、〜

*1 No doubt.は「間違いない」「疑いようもない」というフレーズ。
*2 よくwake (○○) upの形でよく使われる。
　〈例〉I will wake you up at 6:00.　(私はあなたを6時に起こします)
*3 基準となる年の1年前という意味なので、必ずしも「去年」という意味ではない。
　〈例〉I was born in 2008, and he was born the year before.　(私は2008年に生まれ、彼はその1年前に生まれました)
*4 「paper (紙)」「cheese (チーズ)」など不可算名詞を数える時によく使われる。two pieces of 〜 や three pieces of 〜 と複数形にすることも可。
　〈例〉I ate two pieces of cheese.　(私はチーズを2個食べました)

まとめを書こう Review

原級比較 応用編 & 文頭で使われる接続詞

読んでみよう　次の記事を読み、後の問題に答えていきましょう。

Insects Will Save The World

If you are looking for cheap and healthy food, you should try insects. You may think, "What are you thinking? Are you crazy?" But they are not bad at all. Some scientists say no other food is as (1)<u>nutritious</u> as insects because they have a lot of protein, minerals, and vitamins. Insects also have less fat than beef, so it may be a good idea to eat insects instead of beef. (Since hamburgers have too much fat, you should not eat too many of them, but you may be able to eat as many insect burgers as you like.) Some people may think it is strange and only a few people like to eat insects, but that is not true. In fact, *the Food and Agriculture Organization of the United Nations (FAO) says that at least two billion people in the world eat insects as daily food. The world population is now 7.5 billion, so that number is not very low.

Eating insects is not happening only in poor countries. It is happening in high-tech countries, like Japan, too. Let me give you an example. People in Japan eat *inago*, *grasshoppers. Before *World War II, people in the mountain areas often ate *inago*. For example, eating *inago* was pretty common for people in Nagano Prefecture. Why? Because *inago* have high protein, and buying fish and meat was difficult for people in the mountain areas. After World War II, people started using strong *pesticides to kill *inago*, so the number of *inago* decreased. Although finding *inago* in big cities is becoming harder in Japan today, you can still find them at some supermarkets. How do you eat them? Eating them with rice is pretty common, so you can eat them just like you eat beef.

Not only that. Because insects grow faster than cows, producing insects is much easier than producing beef. Why is this important? This is important because the population of the world is increasing. According to *the United Nations, the world population will reach around 10 billion in 2050, and we will face a problem of (2)food shortage. What does that mean? It means we will not have enough food for everyone. In other words, we will need to find ways to produce more food. Many scientists think that we will have less land for farming in the future because of global warming. The high temperature will also cause problems for growing vegetables and plants, so what should we do? Should we produce more beef? I don't think so. Because cows eat a lot of food and drink a lot of water, raising cows is expensive. Some research shows that producing 1 kg of beef needs about 10 kg of food and 20,000 L of water. It also needs a large area because cows are big, so we will lose more food and land if we keep producing beef. How about raising insects? It will not take as much money or land as raising cows, so eating insects is one of the ways to solve this problem. It will also be much easier than developing new technology to produce more food. According to FAO, insects may become our main food in the future. Many companies are interested in this business and some researchers think the market will grow much larger in the next 10 years. If you live in Japan, you may see twice as many *inago* as you see today.

So, we may be able to solve the problem of food shortage by eating insects, but (3)things are not that easy. As you know, accepting the idea of eating insects is difficult for many people. Even though they understand that insects are cheap and nutritious, not that many people will want to see insects on their plates because insects are not yet food for them. If a hamburger restaurant in America sells insect burgers, they will be the least popular food on the menu. If you invite your friends to your place for dinner and serve insects, they may think you are kidding. I won't be surprised if they get angry and decide not to come to your place again.

So, does it mean eating insects will be impossible for us? The answer is "No," because eating strange things is not a new thing. Think about it. People in some Asian countries eat frog, dog, snake, and horse. People in France eat *snail, so we already do eat strange things. We just need to try eating them. They may be delicious. Who knows? Although we cannot imagine yet that we may start seeing insects on our plates more often, I am sure that day will come in the near future. It may happen in the next few years.

I am planning to visit Mexico next month. Why? Because I heard you could eat some insects there. It will be my first time eating insects. I hope I will be able to eat some. (4)Wish me luck!

---

* the Food and Agriculture Organization of the United Nations（FAO）国際連合食糧農業機関　　grasshopper バッタ
World War II 第二次世界大戦　　pesticide 殺虫剤　　the United Nations 国際連合　　snail カタツムリ

問題

Q1. 下線部 (1) の nutritious の意味は次のうちどれか、1つ選びましょう。
1. 栄養がある
2. 値段が安い
3. おいしい
4. すぐに手に入る

Q2. 記事によると世界の人口の約何％が昆虫を食事で食べているか、1つ選びましょう。
1. 約2.7%
2. 約3.75%
3. 約27%
4. 約37.5%

Q3. なぜ長野の人たちは昔よくイナゴを食べていたのか、理由を日本語で2つ書きましょう。

1. _____

2. _____

Q4. 下線部 (2) の food shortage が起きる理由は何か本文から10語以内で抜き出しましょう。

_____

Q5. 牛を育てるのがあまり効率的ではない理由を日本語で2つ書きましょう。

1. _____

2. _____

Q6. なぜ著者は下線部 (3) と言っているのか理由を日本語で書きましょう。

_____

Q7. もし、昆虫が使われたハンバーガーがアメリカのレストランで売られるようになったら、どうなると著者は予想しているか日本語で答えましょう。

_____

Q8. 我々が昆虫を食べるようになるためには、何が必要だと著者は言っているか日本語で答えましょう。

_____

Q9. 下線部（4）のwish me luckは、どういう意味か次の中から1つ選びましょう。
1. 私はロック音楽を聞きにいきます。
2. 私の運は、洗い流されるでしょう。
3. 私はラッキーです。
4. 幸運を祈ってください。

Q10. 次のうち本文に書かれた著者の主張とは異なるものを1つ選びましょう。
1. 第二次世界大戦の後、日本でイナゴの数は減少した。
2. 友だちから昆虫料理を勧められると、昆虫料理が食べやすくなる。
3. 1キロの牛肉を得るのに、牛には10キロの食べ物を与える必要がある。
4. 近い将来、もっと頻繁に昆虫が食卓に並ぶことが予想される。

ここがポイント

今回学ぶのは原級（er / estを足さない形）を使って比較や最上級などを表す方法についてです。以前登場したas 〜 asを応用した形と、"less 〜 than"や"the least"を使った形も学んでいきます。また、sinceやalthoughといった主に文頭で使われる接続詞についても学んでいきます。

1. 原級を使う比較

（1）as 〜 as を使って最上級を表す方法

No (other) ○○ ＋ as 原級 as 〜 ＝「〜ほど…な○○はない」（○○ ＝ 単数形）

〈例〉**No (other) building** in France is **as tall as** this building.

= This building is the tallest in France.

（この建物ほど高い建物はフランスにはありません

= この建物はフランスで一番高いです）

（2）差を具体的に表すas 〜 as

倍数 as 〜 as ＝ ○○倍の〜

〈例〉He has **three times as many English books as** I do.

（彼は私が持っている3倍の数の英語の本を持っています）

> ＊ "倍数 比較級 than"とほとんど同じ意味で使われる。
> He has three times more books than I do.

（3）「好きなだけ〜」「必要なだけ〜」などを表すas 〜 as

as 〜 as ○○ like ＝ ○○が好きなだけ〜

〈例〉He can drink **as much coffee as he likes**.

（彼はコーヒーを好きなだけ飲むことができます）

as 〜 as ○○ want ＝ ○○が欲しいだけ〜 / ○○がしたいだけ〜

〈例〉You can take **as many books as you want**.

（あなたは欲しいだけ本を持っていくことができます）

as 〜 as ○○ need ＝ ○○が必要なだけ〜

〈例〉John can use this computer **as long as he needs**.

（ジョンは必要なだけ長くこのパソコンを使うことができます）

(4) 原級を使って比較を表す方法

less ＋ 原級 ＋ than 〜 ＝「〜ほど…でない」（not as 〜 as とほぼ同じ意味）

〈例〉This car is **less expensive than** that car.

= This car is not as expensive as that car.

（この車はあの車ほど高くはないです）

(5) 原級を使って最上級を表す方法

the least ＋ 原級 ＝「最も…でない」（notは入らないが否定の意味を持つ）

〈例〉This is **the least expensive** computer of the five.

= This is the cheapest computer of the five.

（このパソコンは5つの中で最も高くないパソコンです

= これは5つの中で一番安いパソコンです）

2. 文頭で使う接続詞の基本的な形は「接続詞 ＋ 文, 文」

　文頭で使える接続詞は、基本的に「接続詞 ＋ 文, 文」の形で使います。よく文頭に登場するのは since / although ですが、もうすでに学んだ because / after / before も文頭で使われることがあります。

(1) 文頭で主に使われる接続詞

Since A, B. ＝ A なので B。（A, so B. と同じ意味）

〈例〉**Since** I was tired, I went home early.

= I was tired, so I went home early.

（私は疲れていたので、早く家に帰りました）

> ＊ since は、文の途中で使うことも可能（その際、カンマは不要）。
> 〈例〉I went home early <u>since</u> I was tired.

Although A, B. ＝ A であるが（だけれども）、B。（A, but B. と同じ意味）

〈例〉**Although** she was busy, she went to the party.

= She was busy, but she went to the party.

（彼女は忙しかったのですが、彼女はパーティーに行きました）

> ＊ although と同じ意味で though や even though を使うことができる。
> また、これらは文の途中で使うことも可能（その際、カンマは不要）。
> 〈例〉<u>Though</u> she was busy, she went to the party.
> <u>Even though</u> she was busy, she went to the party.
> She went to the party <u>although</u> she was busy.

(2) 文の途中で主に使われるが、文頭でも使える接続詞

Because A, B. ＝ A なので、B。（A, so B. / Since A, B. と同じ意味）

〈例〉 **Because** I had enough time, I could finish this.

= I had enough time, so I could finish this.

= Since I had enough time, I could finish this.

（私には十分な時間があったので、私はこれを終わらせることができました）

> ＊ Because だけでなく、Because of も文頭で使うことができる。
> 〈例〉 <u>Because of</u> the weather, I couldn't go outside.
> （天気のせいで、私は外に出られませんでした）

After A, B. ＝ A の後で、B。

〈例〉 **After** she finished her homework, she watched TV.

= She watched TV after she finished her homework.

（彼女は宿題を終わらせた後でテレビを見ました）

Before A, B. ＝ A の前に、B。

〈例〉 **Before** you start eating, you should wash your hands.

= You should wash your hands before you start eating.

（あなたは食べ始める前に、手を洗うべきです）

全文の和訳を書いていきましょう。またビデオ講義を
使って音読の練習も行っていきましょう。

1.　Insects Will Save The World

_____

2.　If you are looking for cheap and healthy food, you should try insects.

_____

3.　You may think, "What are you thinking? Are you crazy?" But they are not bad at all.

_____

4.　Some scientists say no other food is as nutritious as insects because they have a lot of
　　protein, minerals, and vitamins.

_____

_____

5.　Insects also have less fat than beef, so it may be a good idea to eat insects instead of
　　beef.

_____

_____

6. (Since hamburgers have too much fat, you should not eat too many of them, but you may be able to eat as many insect burgers as you like.)

_____

_____

7. Some people may think it is strange and only a few people like to eat insects, but that is not true.

_____

_____

8. In fact, the Food and Agriculture Organization of the United Nations (FAO) says that at least two billion people in the world eat insects as daily food.

_____

_____

9. The world population is now 7.5 billion, so that number is not very low.

_____

10. Eating insects is not happening only in poor countries.

_____

11. It is happening in high-tech countries, like Japan, too.

_____

12. Let me give you an example. People in Japan eat _inago_, grasshoppers.

_____

13. Before World War II, people in the mountain areas often ate *inago*.

_____

14. For example, eating *inago* was pretty common for people in Nagano Prefecture.

_____

15. Why? Because *inago* have high protein, and buying fish and meat was difficult for people in the mountain areas.

_____

_____

16. After World War II, people started using strong pesticides to kill *inago*, so the number of *inago* decreased.

_____

_____

17. Although finding *inago* in big cities is becoming harder in Japan today, you can still find them at some supermarkets.

_____

_____

18. How do you eat them?

_____

19. Eating them with rice is pretty common, so you can eat them just like you eat beef.

_____

20.   Not only that. Because insects grow faster than cows, producing insects is much easier than producing beef.

_____

_____

21.   Why is this important?

_____

22.   This is important because the population of the world is increasing.

_____

23.   According to the United Nations, the world population will reach around 10 billion in 2050, and we will face a problem of food shortage.

_____

_____

24.   What does that mean? It means we will not have enough food for everyone.

_____

25.   In other words, we will need to find ways to produce more food.

_____

26.   Many scientists think that we will have less land for farming in the future because of global warming.

_____

_____

27. The high temperature will also cause problems for growing vegetables and plants, so what should we do?

_____

_____

28. Should we produce more beef? I don't think so.

_____

29. Because cows eat a lot of food and drink a lot of water, raising cows is expensive.

_____

30. Some research shows that producing 1 kg of beef needs about 10 kg of food and 20,000 L of water.

_____

_____

31. It also needs a large area because cows are big, so we will lose more food and land if we keep producing beef.

_____

_____

32. How about raising insects?

_____

33. It will not take as much money or land as raising cows, so eating insects is one of the ways to solve this problem.

34. It will also be much easier than developing new technology to produce more food.

35. According to FAO, insects may become our main food in the future.

36. Many companies are interested in this business and some researchers think the market will grow much larger in the next 10 years.

37. If you live in Japan, you may see twice as many *inago* as you see today.

38. So, we may be able to solve the problem of food shortage by eating insects, but things are not that easy.

39. As you know, accepting the idea of eating insects is difficult for many people.

40. Even though they understand that insects are cheap and nutritious, not that many people will want to see insects on their plates because insects are not yet food for them.

_____

_____

_____

41. If a hamburger restaurant in America sells insect burgers, they will be the least popular food on the menu.

_____

_____

42. If you invite your friends to your place for dinner and serve insects, they may think you are kidding.

_____

_____

43. I won't be surprised if they get angry and decide not to come to your place again.

_____

44. So, does it mean eating insects will be impossible for us?

_____

45. The answer is "No," because eating strange things is not a new thing.

_____

46. Think about it. People in some Asian countries eat frog, dog, snake, and horse.

_____

47. People in France eat snail, so we already do eat strange things.

_____

48. We just need to try eating them. They may be delicious. Who knows?

_____

49. Although we cannot imagine yet that we may start seeing insects on our plates more often, I am sure that day will come in the near future.

_____

_____

50. It may happen in the next few years.

_____

51. I am planning to visit Mexico next month.

_____

52. Why? Because I heard you could eat some insects there.

_____

53. It will be my first time eating insects. I hope I will be able to eat some. Wish me luck!

_____

語句の確認

Mexico	【名(固有)】メキシコ
vitamin	【名(可算・通常複数形)】ビタミン
plate	【名(可算)】(浅くて丸い)皿
population	【名(不可算・具体的には可算)】人口
beef	【名(不可算)】牛肉
mineral	【名(不可算・具体的には可算)】ミネラル
protein	【名(不可算・種類には可算)】たんぱく質/プロテイン
farm	【名(可算)】農場/農園 【動】(畑を)耕す/農業する
research	【名(不可算)】研究/リサーチ 【動】研究する/調査する
fat	【名(不可算)】脂肪/脂質 【形】太っている

accept	【動】受け入れる/引き受ける
reach	【動】届く/着く/到着する/達する
produce	【動】生産する/製造する
develop	【動】開発する/発達させる
increase	【動】増える/増加する
decrease	【動】減少する/低下する
nutritious	【形】栄養のある
billion	【形】10億の
common	【形】一般的な/普通の/共通の
strange	【形】奇妙な/不思議な/変な
daily	【形】毎日の/日常の 【副】毎日
according to ～	【熟】～によると/～によれば

まとめを書こう

まとめのテスト

読んでみよう　　次の記事を読み、後の問いに答えましょう。

Sleep well and eat breakfast if you want to get good grades!

If you are a student, do you want to improve your grades? If you answered yes, let me ask you two more questions. How many hours do you sleep every day? Do you eat breakfast every morning? You may think "Why are you asking these questions? Why do they matter?" so I will tell you the reasons. I asked those questions because you can improve your grades by sleeping well and eating breakfast, but don't get me wrong. I am not saying you do not have to study hard to get good grades. I am saying sleeping well and eating breakfast are as important as studying hard.

<Sleeping>

So, how many hours do we need to sleep? Many scientists agree that students should sleep around eight hours every day. (Older people usually sleep less, so it is OK if your parents sleep less than eight hours.) If you get enough sleep, you will not feel sleepy or tired, so you will be able to (1)concentrate on studying. Not only that; some research shows that the number of mistakes will decrease if we sleep well. What does that mean? That means studying without sleeping is bad. Some students study all night before their tests, but that is not a good idea. If you want to get good scores on your tests, you should not try to cover everything on the day before.

However, sleeping for about eight hours every day is difficult for many high school students. It is not because they are lazy. It is because they are facing many changes in their lives. For example, they usually get much more homework than elementary or junior high school students do. If they are playing sports or working part-time, they will have to do their homework after they finish those. In addition, Social Networking Services (SNS) can also cause some problems, so some students

178

may always feel tired, and getting enough sleep will become difficult for them.

Sleeping will also make your body stronger and healthier. One research study shows that you may *gain weight if you do not sleep well, so getting enough sleep is very important. However, it is difficult for many students, so we need to do something. One of the ways to improve this is to change the school schedule. It sounds challenging, but some researchers in America and England are trying to make this happen. Because many high school students in America have to be at school before 8:00 a.m., some researchers are trying to change it to 8:30 a.m. or later. Some researchers in England say high schools should start at 10:00 a.m. because students are too tired. They think these changes will make students' school life more *meaningful.

<Eating Breakfast>

Now, let's talk about breakfast. Do you eat breakfast every morning? Eating breakfast is as important as sleeping well. Many scientists believe breakfast is the most important meal of the day because it gives you energy and tells your body to wake up. If you are a student, eating breakfast will be a great way to start your day because it will give you enough energy to get through your morning classes. In fact, many scientists agree that there is a strong *relationship between eating breakfast and students' grades. In other words, you should eat breakfast if you want to get good grades. Eating breakfast will also change your mood, and some data show that (2)skipping breakfast will make you fat because you will eat more at night, so if you want to have a great school life, eating a good breakfast is very important.

However, some children in Japan do not eat breakfast before they go to school, and it is becoming a serious problem. According to *MEXT, about 5% of 6th graders and about 8% of 3rd year junior high school students do not eat breakfast. What are the reasons? Many students say they are not hungry or do not have enough time to eat breakfast in the morning. Although the numbers are still low, they are increasing, so we must find a way to stop it.

As I said, eating breakfast is very important, but it does not mean you can eat anything for breakfast. Eating nutritious food is the best, so you should not eat snacks for breakfast. You should eat vegetables and fruit because they have a lot of vitamins and minerals. Eating eggs and yogurt is also good because you can get protein. You also need *carbohydrates, so don't forget to eat rice or bread.

I know that preparing this kind of breakfast sounds hard, but providing a nutritious breakfast is very important for students' learning, so, who is going to prepare it? My answer is "parents." If parents want their children to learn well and get good grades, they must support their children by providing a good breakfast because children usually do not have time to make one in the morning. Because parents cannot go to class and take tests for their children, making a good breakfast is an important way to support their children.

Many parents tell their children to study hard if their grades are bad, but maybe just telling them to study hard will not solve the problem if they are not getting enough sleep or a good breakfast. If you are a parent and not happy with your child's grades, I want to ask you two questions: Is your child getting enough sleep? And, do you make a good breakfast for him or her?

* gain 増す/手に入れる　　meaningful 意味のある/有意義な　　relationship 関係　　MEXT 文部科学省
carbohydrate 炭水化物

問　題

Q1. 熱心に勉強をすること以外に、成績を上げるのに必要なことを日本語で2つ答えましょう。

1. _____　　2. _____

Q2. 下線部 (1) の concentrate は日本語でどういう意味になるか、一番意味の近い選択肢を選びましょう。
1. お金を使う　　　2. 集中する　　　3. 適当に行う　　　4. 質問する

Q3. 高校生にとって十分な時間寝るのが難しい理由として<u>間違っているもの</u>を1つ選びましょう。
1. アルバイトをしているかもしれないから。
2. SNSなどでの問題を抱えているかもしれないから。
3. 怠慢になる傾向があるから。
4. 学校の宿題が多いから。

Q4. 高校生が十分な睡眠時間を確保できるように、西洋の国々が議論している対策は何か、日本語で答えましょう。

_____

Q5. 朝食がもたらす効果として本文に書かれているものには○、書かれていないものには×を（　）に書いていきましょう。

1. 気分を良くしてくれる。　（　　　）

2. 体を起こしてくれる。　（　　　）

3. 疲労を回復させる。　（　　　）

4. 夜の寝つきを良くしてくれる。　（　　　）

Q6. 下線部（2）のskipping breakfastは、ここではどういう意味で使われているか、一番意味の近い選択肢を選びましょう。

1. 朝食後にスキップすること

2. 朝食の前に軽い運動をすること

3. 朝食にスキップという料理を食べること

4. 朝食を抜くこと

Q7. 日本で朝食を食べない小・中学生の多くが、朝食を食べない理由としてあげていることを、日本語で2つ答えましょう。

1. _____

2. _____

Q8. 次のうち、著者が最も勧めるであろう朝食の組み合わせはどれでしょう。

1. たまご入りサラダ/トースト/ヨーグルト

2. 味噌汁/ご飯/漬物

3. コーンフレーク/菓子パン

4. ドーナツ/コーヒー

Q9. 著者は、栄養のある朝食を用意するのは誰の仕事だと主張しているか、日本語で答えましょう。

_____

Q10. 本文の内容とは<u>異なるもの</u>を1つ選びましょう。

    1. 試験の前日に徹夜して勉強をするのは、あまり効果的な勉強法とは言えない。

    2. 多くの科学者は、夕食の次に朝食は重要な食事であると考えている。

    3. 大人にとっての理想の睡眠時間は一般的に8時間よりも短い。

    4. 日本の中学3年生は、小学6年生より朝食を食べない傾向にある。

全文の和訳を書いていきましょう。またビデオ講義を使って音読の練習も行っていきましょう。

1.   Sleep well and eat breakfast if you want to get good grades!

2.   If you are a student, do you want to improve your grades?

3.   If you answered yes, let me ask you two more questions.

4.   How many hours do you sleep every day? Do you eat breakfast every morning?

5.   You may think "Why are you asking these questions? Why do they matter?" so I will tell you the reasons.

6. I asked those questions because you can improve your grades by sleeping well and eating breakfast, but don't get me wrong.

_____

_____

7. I am not saying you do not have to study hard to get good grades.

_____

8. I am saying sleeping well and eating breakfast are as important as studying hard.

_____

9. <Sleeping> So, how many hours do we need to sleep?

_____

10. Many scientists agree that students should sleep around eight hours every day.

_____

11. (Older people usually sleep less, so it is OK if your parents sleep less than eight hours.)

_____

_____

12. If you get enough sleep, you will not feel sleepy or tired, so you will be able to concentrate on studying.

_____

_____

13. Not only that; some research shows that the number of mistakes will decrease if we sleep well.

14. What does that mean? That means studying without sleeping is bad.

15. Some students study all night before their tests, but that is not a good idea.

16. If you want to get good scores on your tests, you should not try to cover everything on the day before.

17. However, sleeping for about eight hours every day is difficult for many high school students.

18. It is not because they are lazy.

19. It is because they are facing many changes in their lives.

20. For example, they usually get much more homework than elementary or junior high school students do.

_____

_____

21. If they are playing sports or working part-time, they will have to do their homework after they finish those.

_____

_____

22. In addition, Social Networking Services (SNS) can also cause some problems, so some students may always feel tired, and getting enough sleep will become difficult for them.

_____

_____

_____

23. Sleeping will also make your body stronger and healthier.

_____

24. One research study shows that you may gain weight if you do not sleep well, so getting enough sleep is very important.

_____

_____

25. However, it is difficult for many students, so we need to do something.

_____

26. One of the ways to improve this is to change the school schedule.

_____

27. It sounds challenging, but some researchers in America and England are trying to make this happen.

_____

_____

28. Because many high school students in America have to be at school before 8:00 a.m., some researchers are trying to change it to 8:30 a.m. or later.

_____

_____

29. Some researchers in England say high schools should start at 10:00 a.m. because students are too tired.

_____

_____

30. They think these changes will make students' school life more meaningful.

_____

31. <Eating Breakfast> Now, let's talk about breakfast. Do you eat breakfast every morning?

_____

_____

32. Eating breakfast is as important as sleeping well.

_____

33. Many scientists believe breakfast is the most important meal of the day because it gives you energy and tells your body to wake up.

_____

_____

34. If you are a student, eating breakfast will be a great way to start your day because it will give you enough energy to get through your morning classes.

_____

_____

35. In fact, many scientists agree that there is a strong relationship between eating breakfast and students' grades.

_____

_____

36. In other words, you should eat breakfast if you want to get good grades.

_____

37. Eating breakfast will also change your mood, and some data show that skipping breakfast will make you fat because you will eat more at night, so if you want to have a great school life, eating a good breakfast is very important.

_____

_____

_____

38. However, some children in Japan do not eat breakfast before they go to school, and it is becoming a serious problem.

_____

_____

39. According to MEXT, about 5% of 6th graders and about 8% of 3rd year junior high school students do not eat breakfast.

_____

_____

40. What are the reasons?

_____

41. Many students say they are not hungry or do not have enough time to eat breakfast in the morning.

_____

_____

42. Although the numbers are still low, they are increasing, so we must find a way to stop it.

_____

_____

43. As I said, eating breakfast is very important, but it does not mean you can eat anything for breakfast.

_____

_____

44. Eating nutritious food is the best, so you should not eat snacks for breakfast.

_____

45. You should eat vegetables and fruit because they have a lot of vitamins and minerals.

_____

46. Eating eggs and yogurt is also good because you can get protein.

_____

47. You also need carbohydrates, so don't forget to eat rice or bread.

_____

48. I know that preparing this kind of breakfast sounds hard, but providing a nutritious breakfast is very important for students' learning, so, who is going to prepare it?

_____

_____

29.   My answer is "parents."

_____

50.   If parents want their children to learn well and get good grades, they must support their children by providing a good breakfast because children usually do not have time to make one in the morning.

_____

_____

_____

51.   Because parents cannot go to class and take tests for their children, making a good breakfast is an important way to support their children.

_____

_____

52.   Many parents tell their children to study hard if their grades are bad, but maybe just telling them to study hard will not solve the problem if they are not getting enough sleep or a good breakfast.

_____

_____

_____

53. If you are a parent and not happy with your child's grades, I want to ask you two questions: Is your child getting enough sleep? And, do you make a good breakfast for him or her?

_____

_____

_____

まとめを書こう

Review

藤井 拓哉
ふじい たくや

1984年生まれ。父親の仕事の都合で3歳〜6歳までと、15歳〜24歳までをアメリカのオハイオ州で過ごす。オハイオ州立大学、同大学院で教育学を学び、日本語の教員免許とTESOL（英語を母国語としない方のための英語教授法）を取得。帰国後は、宇都宮大学で英語講師を務める。数学、化学、生物学、物理学を英語で学ぶ「理数系英語」の講義を定期的に行い、2010年と2013年にベストレクチャー賞を受賞。現在は、筑波技術大学で英語講師を務める。著書に『たくや式中学英語ノート』シリーズ全10巻、『たくや式どんどん読める中学英語長文』シリーズ（どちらも朝日学生新聞社）、『MP3CD 付きガチトレ　英語スピーキング徹底トレーニング』シリーズ（ベレ出版）。TOEIC955 点、TOEFL101点。

https://withyoufujii.com　ツイッター：@gachitore1

英文校閲	Jack Stowers
イラスト	きつまき
デザイン	村上史恵
編集	佐藤夏理　高見澤恵理

たくや式 どんどん読める 中学英語長文 4
中2　比較

2021年6月30日　初版第一刷発行

著者	藤井拓哉
発行者	清田哲
発行所	朝日学生新聞社
	〒104–8433　東京都中央区築地5–3–2　朝日新聞社新館9階
	電話03–3545–5436
	www.asagaku.jp（朝日学生新聞社の出版物案内）
印刷所	株式会社シナノパブリッシングプレス

©Takuya Fujii 2021 Printed in Japan
ISBN 978–4–909876–14–0

どんどん読める

中学英語

長文 **4**

中2 比較

解答編

別冊

本冊と軽くのりづけされています。
取り外してお使いください。

朝日学生新聞社

1 基礎力確認テスト

(p.8)

解答例

Q1. (A) to come　(B) shopping　(C) doing
　　(D) to practice　(E) taking

Q2. 4

Q3. Because she is in a music band, and her
band is (they are) going to have a concert
at Sakura Hall next month.

Q4. Many / were / there / weren't

Q5. 3

Q6. 2

Q7. 2

Q8. 7本

Q9. サクラホールの（後ろの）駐車場

Q10. 3

解説

Q1. (A) planは目的語にto不定詞を取る動詞。
(B) 前置詞 (for) の後には動名詞が入る。
(C) 過去進行形の疑問文なので、ingの形。
(D) beginは、動名詞とto不定詞の両方とも
目的語に取れる動詞。ただし、to practicing
は「to＋動名詞」なので×。
(E) 前置詞（without）の後には動名詞が入る。

Q2. 問題は「サツキは学校に来るのにどれくらい
時間がかかったでしょう」という意味。本文
序盤にサツキが、it took an hour and a half
for me to get here（私がここまで来るのに1
時間半かかったよ）と説明している。

Q3. 問題は「なぜグレースはピアノを練習する必
要があったのでしょう」という意味。本文序
盤サツキの、Why did you need to practice
that long?（なんで、そんなに長い間、練習を
する必要があったの）という質問に対しグレー
スが、Because I'm in a music band, and
we are going to have a concert at Sakura
Hall next month.（〈なぜなら〉私は音楽バン
ドに入っていて、私たちは来月サクラホール
でコンサートを行う予定だからだ）と答え
ている。

Q4. 「人」は可算名詞のため、最初のカッコには
manyが入る。「立っていました」は、過去進
行形なので、be動詞の過去形＋動詞ingの形。
主語がmany peopleなので2つ目のカッコに
はwereが入る。
「～がない」は、there＋be動詞＋notの形
で表すことができる。「十分な数の座席」と複
数の可算名詞で過去のことなので、there
were notの形が必要なのだが、カッコが2つ
しかないため、there weren't となる。

Q5. 本文中盤のグレースの、Will you have time
on December 26th?（12月26日に時間はあ
る?）という質問に対しサツキが、I think so.
～. Why?（あると思うよ。～。なんで?）と
答えた後、we are planning to take all our
instruments there on that day. My job is to
take eight guitars to the concert hall, ～.
Will you help me?（私たちは、我々の全て
の楽器をその日にそこに持っていく予定なの。
私の仕事は、コンサートホールに8本のギタ
ーを持っていくことで、～。助けてくれない
かな?）と答えている。

Q6. このmap（地図）は、グレースが描いたサク
ラホールの場所を表す地図。本文中盤でグレー
スが、It is on Kasama Street. Do you
know the park near the station? Sakura
Hall is in front of the park. I think there is a
parking area behind the concert hall（カサ
マ通りにあるんだ。駅の近くの公園は知って
いる?　サクラホールはその正面だよ。駐車
場がコンサートホールの後ろにあると思う）、
I think the name of the park is Motegi Park
（モテギ公園だと思う）と説明している。
また、Fujishiro Park is on Tomei Street and
a little bit far from the station.（フジシロ公
園は、トメイ通りにあって駅からは少し遠い
んだ）と説明している。

Q7. 下線部 (3) のthisについてサツキが、What is
it?（それは何?）と質問した直後にグレースが、
It is a ticket to park your car.（あなたの車を
止めるためのチケットだよ）と説明している。

Q8. 本文中盤でグレースが、My job is to take

eight guitars to the concert hall, (私の仕事は、コンサートホールに8本のギターを持っていくこと) と書かれているが本文最後で、I want you to take these seven guitars. (私はこれらの7本のギターを持っていってもらいたいの) と本数が変わっているので注意。

Q9. 最後から2番目のグレースの発言に、After you finish, you can go to the concert hall. I hope to see you in the parking area. (終わったら、コンサートホールに向かってもらってかまわないから。駐車場で会えることを望むよ) と書かれている。

Q10. 本文中盤で、グレースが12月26日の待ち合わせ場所について、Let's meet in front of Building C. (C棟の前で会いましょう) と発言し、当日2人が会ってからのサツキのIs it far from here? (ここから遠いの?) という発言に対しグレースが、No, it's not. (いいや、遠くないよ) と発言しているため、正解は3.

1. は、本文序盤にグレースが、Do you come to school by car every day? (毎日車で学校に来ているの?) と質問し、サツキが、Yeah. (うん) と答えている。

2. は、本文中盤でグレースが、Will you have time on December 26th? (12月26日に時間はある?) とサツキに聞いた後で、It is the day before our concert (私たちのコンサートの前日で) と発言しているため、コンサートは12月27日だと分かる。

4. は、本文中盤でグレースが、Will you have time on December 26th? (12月26日に時間はある?) とサツキに聞いた後でサツキが、I will have time after my math class. (数学の授業の後なら時間があるでしょう) と答えている。

全文和訳例

1. サツキ:どうも、グレース。調子はどう?
2. グレース:こんにちは、サツキ。今ここに着いたの?
3. サツキ:いいえ。10:30に授業があったから、10:20頃にここに来たよ。
4. 9:30頃にここに来る予定だったんだ。(なぜなら) 授業の前に図書館から本を何冊か借りたかったから。だけど、道がとても混雑していたから、私がここまで来るのに1時間半かかったよ。
5. グレース:毎日車で学校に来ているの?
6. サツキ:うん。母親の車なんだけど、毎日使っているんだ。(なぜなら) 母親 (彼女) は週末の買い物のためにしか車 (それ) を使わないから。
7. 午前中に何か授業はあったの?
8. グレース:いいえ。
9. サツキ:それじゃあ、何をしていたの?
10. グレース:えっと、私は11時までピアノの練習をしていたんだ。
11. 9時に練習を始めたから、けっこう長かったね。
12. 休みを取らずに2時間練習するのは、とても大変だったよ。
13. サツキ:うわぁ。なんで、そんなに長い間、練習をする必要があったの?
14. グレース:(なぜなら) 私は音楽バンドに入っていて、私たちは来月サクラホールでコンサートを行う予定だからだよ。
15. 私たちは、去年もコンサートを行って、とても良かったんだ。
16. たくさんの人たちが、私たちの音楽を聴くのを楽しんだと思う。
17. サツキ:たくさんの人がコンサートにはいたの?
18. グレース:うん、いたよ。
19. 多くの人は立っていたんだ。(なぜなら) 十分な数の席がなかったから。
20. サツキ:うわぁ。なるほどね。
21. グレース:あぁ、質問があるんだ。12月26日に時間はある?
22. 金曜日で、冬休み前の最後の学校の日だけど。
23. サツキ:あると思うよ。数学の授業の後なら時間があるでしょう。
24. 1:00に始まって2:30に終わるから、その後なら時間があると思うよ。なんで?
25. グレース:えっと、(なぜなら) 誰か私を助け

てくれないか探していてね。

26. 私たちのコンサートの前日で、私たちは、我々の全ての楽器をその日にそこに持っていく予定なの。

27. 私の仕事は、コンサートホールに8本のギターを持っていくことで、それらは私のではないんだ。

28. 大きくて重たいから、それらを車で持っていきたいんだけど、私は車を持っていなくて。助けてくれないかな？

29. サツキ：もちろん。サクラホールにギターを持っていってもらいたいの？

30. グレース：うん。

31. サツキ：オーケー。できると思うよ。だけど、私の車はとても小さいから、あなたが乗るための十分なスペースはないだろうね。

32. グレース：それは、大丈夫。私は電車に乗って歩いてコンサートホールに行けるから。

33. サツキ：オーケー。コンサートホールはどこなの？

34. グレース：カサマ通りにあるんだ。駅の近くの公園は知っている？

35. サクラホールはその正面だよ。

36. 駐車場がコンサートホールの後ろにあると思うから、そこにあなたの車を止めることができるでしょう。

37. サツキ：どの公園について言っているの？

38. フジシロ公園について言っているの？

39. グレース：いいえ。そっちじゃないね。

40. フジシロ公園は、トメイ通りにあって駅からは少し遠いんだ。

41. 公園の名前は、モテギ公園だと思うけど、確かではないかな。

42. 大きいから、見逃さないと思うよ。

43. サツキ：地図を描いてくれる？

44. グレース：もちろん。それは良いアイデアだね。紙とペンは持っている？

45. サツキ：うん、持っているよ。これを使っていいよ。

46. グレース：ありがとう。
（5分後）

47. グレース：オーケー。これが地図。駅からそ

こに着くのはとても簡単だよ。

48. あぁ、待って。これを持っていく必要があるよ。

49. サツキ：それは何？

50. グレース：あなたの車を止めるためのチケットだよ。

51. このチケットなしではあなたの車を止めることができないんだ。

52. サツキ：オーケー。ありがとう。何時に私にギターを取りに来てほしいの？

53. グレース：そうだね。2：00から会議があって、長さは1時間だから、3：30に会える？

54. サツキ：いいね。どこで会いたい？

55. グレース：C棟の前で会いましょう。

56. そこから、私たちの練習部屋に連れていけるから。

57. サツキ：オーケー。いいね。あ、ごめん。授業に行く時間だ。またね。

58. グレース：オーケー。授業楽しんで。
（12月26日）

59. サツキ：こんにちは、グレース。

60. グレース：やあ、サツキ。今日は手伝ってくれてありがとう。

61. オーケー。練習部屋に行きましょう。

62. サツキ：ここから遠いの？

63. グレース：いいや、遠くないよ。そこに着くまでに2分ぐらいしか、かからないと思うよ。だけど、説明するのが難しくて。（なぜなら）何回も曲がる必要があるからね。
（練習部屋にて）

64. グレース：オーケー。これらがそのギターです。あなたの車に運び始めてくれる？

65. 終わったら、コンサートホールに向かってもらってかまわないから。

66. 駐車場で会えることを望むよ。

67. サツキ：いいね。この黒いギターも持っていってほしいの？

68. グレース：いいや。それは大丈夫。

69. それは使わないって、私たちは決めたんだ。だから、私はこれらの7本のギターを持っていってもらいたいの。

70. サツキ：わかったよ。

2 新しい助動詞

解答例

Q1. 1. ○ 2. × 3. ○ 4. ×

Q2. （少し遠いため）エマの1時の会議に間に合いそうにないから。

Q3. ウェブサイトにレストランを高く評価するコメントがたくさん書いてあったから。

Q4. it was raining (outside).

Q5. 3

Q6. 1

Q7. 4

Q8. 会議で説明することが書かれたリストを覚えること

Q9. (They need to) press the button on the table.

Q10. 2

解説

Q1. 1.は、本文序盤にエマがカレーゴーゴーについて、we go there a lot（私たちがよく行く）と発言しているので○。

2.は、本文序盤にジョンが、How about Olio? It is an Italian restaurant near Akatsuka Gym.（オリオはどう？ アカツカ体育館の近くにあるイタリアンレストラン）と説明しているので×。

3.は、本文序盤にエマが、I want to take my family there sometime（いつか家族を連れていきたいと思っているんだ）と説明しているので○。

4.は、本文中盤にジョンがジョージョー（Jyo-Jyo）の説明として、It is a new restaurant.（新しいレストランだよ）と説明しているので×。

Q2. 本文序盤、ジョンがオリオについて、It is a little bit far from here（ここから少しだけ遠い）と説明している。また、その次のエマの発言で、We cannot go to that restaurant because I have a meeting from one.（私たちはそのレストランに行けないな。〈なぜなら〉1時から会議があるから）と説明している。

Q3. 下線部（2）は「（彼らは）おいしい食べ物を出すに違いない」という意味。本文中盤、ジョンがジョージョーについてのウェブサイトを見ている時に、look at all these positive comments（これら全てのポジティブなコメントを見て）と発言している。

Q4. 問題は「なぜジョンとエマは車でレストランに行くことを決めたのでしょう？」という意味。本文中盤でジョンが、It is raining outside. Should we go by car?（外は雨が降っているね。車で行くべきかな？）という発言に対しエマがSure. I don't want to walk in the rain. Let's go by car.（そうだね。雨の中歩きたくはないから。車で行きましょう）と答えている。

Q5. 1.は「昨日は、あなたはここに来ることができませんでした」

2.は「ごめんなさい。私たちには空いている席が全くないです」

3.は「テーブルを確認する必要があります」

4.は「車を止めることはできましたか？」

直前でエマが、Is this the waiting list? Do I have to write my name here?（これは、ウェイティングリストですか？ 私は、名前をここに書かないといけないのですか？）と発言し、ウェイターが、Could you wait for a second?（少々お待ちいただけますか？）と発言し、（ア）の直後に、Oh, you don't have to write your name.（あぁ、〈あなたは〉名前を書かないで大丈夫です）と発言していることから、（ア）でテーブルの空きがあるか確認していたことが分かる。

Q6. 本文中盤、ジョンとエマがレストランで席に着いた際エマが、This table is nice. I like this big window because I can see outside. It is close to the kitchen, too.（このテーブルは素敵だね。この大きな窓がいいね、〈なぜなら〉外が見られるから。キッチンにも近いし）と発言している。

Q7. 何を食べるかを選ぶ際エマが、We do not have much time（私たちには時間がありません）、I don't want to eat soup or noodles

6

because I may get a stain. (スープや麺類は食べたくないです。〈なぜなら〉シミが付くかもしれないので)、I don't want to eat garlic, either (ニンニクも食べたくないです)、no curry (カレーもなしで) と発言している。

Q8. 下線部 (3) の this の少し前でエマが、I have to explain many things during the meeting today, and this is the list. (今日の会議でたくさんのことを説明しないといけなくて、これがそのリスト)、I must remember them because I must not look at the memo when I explain these things. (これらを覚えなくちゃいけなくて。〈なぜなら〉これらを説明する際、私はメモを見てはいけないから) と発言しており、下線部 (3) のところで、but I think I will get nervous and forget everything, so this may not help me at all. (だけど、緊張して全て忘れちゃうだろうから、これは全く私の助けにならないかも) と発言していることから、this は「リスト」ではなく「リストを覚えること」だというのが分かる。

Q9. 問題は「エマとジョンが食事の後でデザートを得るためには、何をする必要があるでしょう?」という意味。本文終盤でウェイターが、I will bring your desserts after you finish your meals. Do you see that button on the table? You can press that to let me know. (食事の後にデザートをお持ちします。テーブル上のあのボタンが見えますか? あれを押して私に知らせてください) と発言している。

Q10. 1.は、本文中盤でジョンが、I thought you smoked. (タバコを吸わなかったっけ) と発言し、直後にエマが Well, I do, but ～ (まぁ、吸うけど、～) と発言している。
3.は、本文終盤エマが飲み物とデザートを頼む際、I will have coffee and vanilla ice cream for my dessert. (私はコーヒーと、デザートにバニラアイスをお願いします) と発言し、直後にジョンが I'll have the same. (私も同じので) と発言している。
4.は、本文中盤、パソコンでレストランを探している際、ジョージョーについてジョンが

It is only 300 meters away from here. (ここから 300m しか離れていないよ) と発言している。

全文和訳例

1. エマ:どうも、ジョン。今日は昼食にどこに行きたい?
2. ジョン:わかんないな。昨日はどこに行ったっけ?
3. エマ:大通り (メインストリート) にあるカレーレストラン。
4. 名前は忘れちゃったんだけど、私たちがよく行く。
5. ジョン:あぁ、カレーゴーゴーだ。
6. エマ:それだ。どこかに書いておかないと。(なぜなら) 覚えられないから。
7. いつか家族を (そこに) 連れていきたいと思っているんだ。(なぜなら) カレーがおいしいし、たくさんのサラダとナンがついてくるから。
8. ジョン:そうだね。知っている。そうするべきだよ。あなたの家族が大いに気に入るのは確かだね。
9. 前回の週末に妻とそこに行ったんだけど、彼女はカレーを本当に堪能していたよ。
10. エマ:彼女は全て食べることができたの?
11. ジョン:いいや、できなかったね。彼女にとっては多すぎる量の食べ物だったから。
12. それはさておき、今日はカレーゴーゴーに行くのはやめておきましょう。
13. エマ:オーケー。どこに私たちは行くべきかな?
14. (私たちは) 毎日外に出て昼食を取るから、新しい選択肢はないかもね。
15. ジョン:どれどれ。オリオはどう?
16. アカツカ体育館の近くにあるイタリアンレストラン。
17. ここから少しだけ遠いけど、ピザがとてもおいしいよ。
18. 1時までには戻って来られると思うし。どう思う?
19. エマ:うん。いいね。あ、待って。
20. 私たちはそのレストランに行けないな。(なぜ

なら）1時から会議があるから。

21. そのことを忘れていたよ。ごめん。

22. ジョン：何時に戻って来たいの？

23. エマ：12：50までには戻ってきたいな。（なぜなら）準備をするための時間が必要かもしれないから。

24. ジョン：オーケー。じゃあ、私たちはレストランを早く選ばないといけないね。いくつか調べてみるよ。
（パソコンでいくつかのレストランを調べている）

25. ジョン：これはどう？　イナバ公園の近くのファミリーレストラン。

26. ここから300mしか離れていないよ。

27. エマ：この辺にファミリーレストランがあるなんて知らなかったよ。

28. 名前は何？

29. ジョン：ジョージョー。新しいレストランだよ。このウェブサイトによると1か月前にオープンしたばかりなんだけど、これら全てのポジティブなコメントを見て。

30. エマ：おやまぁ。信じられない。（彼らは）おいしい食べ物を出すに違いない。

31. 混んでいないことを願うよ。

32. ジョン：外は雨が降っているね。車で行くべきかな？

33. エマ：そうだね。雨の中歩きたくはないから。車で行きましょう。
（レストランにて）

34. エマ：わぁ。私たちはラッキーだね。今日は、そんなにたくさんの人はいないね。

35. ジョン：そうだね。天気があまりよくないから、多分それが原因だね。

36. ウェイター：お手伝いしましょうか？

37. エマ：あぁ、はい。これは、ウェイティングリストですか？　私は、名前をここに書かないといけないのですか？

38. ウェイター：少々お待ちいただけますか？　テーブルを確認する必要があります。

39. あぁ、（あなたは）名前を書かないで大丈夫です。何名様ですか？

40. エマ：2人だけです。

41. ウェイター：喫煙・禁煙どちらですか？

42. エマ：禁煙でお願いします。

43. ウェイター：オーケー。私についてきてください。

44. ジョン：タバコを吸わなかったっけ（あなたはタバコを吸うと思ったけど）。

45. エマ：まぁ、吸うけど、今日は昼食後にタバコを吸うのを楽しむための十分な時間は私たちにはないと思うから。
（テーブルにて）

46. エマ：このテーブルは素敵だね。この大きな窓がいいね、（なぜなら）外が見られるから。

47. キッチンにも近いし。

48. ジョン：そうだね。メニューを見てみよう…わぁ。全てとてもおいしそうに見えるね。

49. エマ：覚えておいて。私たちはかなり急いで食べないといけないんだからね。

50. ウェイター：ご注文を伺ってもよろしいですか？

51. エマ：ええっと。あなたの助けが必要です。私たちには時間がありません。（なぜなら）ここを30分で出ないといけないので。

52. そして、私はスープや麺類は食べたくないです。（なぜなら）シミが付くかもしれないので。

53. ニンニクも食べたくないです。（なぜなら）午後に会議があるので。

54. あぁ、あとカレーもなしで。（なぜなら）昨日食べたので。そうすると、私は何を食べるべきでしょう？

55. ウェイター：当店の（私たちの）焼き鮭はいかがでしょう？

56. （私たちは）10分でご用意できると思います。

57. サラダ、飲み物、デザートがついてきます。そして、たったの800円です。

58. エマ：いいですね。それにします。

59. ジョン：それは本当にいいですね。私もそれにします。

60. ウェイター：オーケー。飲み物とデザートは何がよろしいですか？

61. メニューの裏にリストがあります。

62. エマ：私はコーヒーと、デザートにバニラアイスをお願いします。

63. ジョン：私も同じので。
（ウェイターが去る）

64. ジョン：何を読んでいるの？

65. エマ：あぁ、これ？　今日の会議でたくさんのことを説明しないといけなくて、これがそのリスト。

66. これらを覚えなくちゃいけなくて。（なぜなら）これらを説明する際、私はメモを見てはいけないから。

67. ジョン：どうしてダメなの？

68. エマ：えぇっと、（なぜなら）私の上司がそう言うから。

69. 前回、メモを見て我々のスケジュールについて話したんだけど、私の上司はそれが気に入らなかったんだ。

70. 彼は、私は真っすぐ立って、はっきり話すべきだと思っていて。

71. 彼には全く同意なんだけど、私にとってそれをするのはとても難しくてね。

72. 今私はリストをチェックしているんだけど、緊張して全て忘れちゃうだろうから、これは全く私の助けにならないかも。
（ウェイターが料理を持ってくる）

73. ウェイター：オーケー。どうぞ。

74. ジョン：ありがとうございます。素晴らしいですね。

75. ウェイター：食事の後にデザートをお持ちします。

76. テーブル上のあのボタンが見えますか？　あれを押して私に知らせてください。

77. 食事を楽しんで。

78. エマ＆ジョン：ありがとうございます。
（彼らが食事を終えて）

79. ジョン：私は（食べ）終わったよ。とてもおいしかったね。鮭とデザートが本当に気に入ったよ。

80. また、私たちは来るべきだね。

81. エマ：そうだね。私はデザートが気に入ったね。アイスはとてもおいしかった。

82. オーケー。何時ですか？

83. ジョン：12：45なので、もう私たちは戻る必要があるね。行きましょうか？

84. エマ：そうだね。

3 　be動詞の原形と接続詞 if / when / that

(p.44)

解答例

Q1.　(She wanted to be a) singer / idol (.)

Q2.　(She studied) journalism (.)

Q3.　1. ◯　2. ×　3. ◯　4. ×

Q4.　YouTuber

Q5.　次のうちの2つ。

　　・お金を稼ぐのが難しい。（有名になるまで貧しい暮らしをしないといけないかもしれない）

　　・（みんなが見る動画を作るために）創造力がないといけない。

　　・（毎日）撮影、編集、アップロードを自分で行わないといけない。（夏休み・冬休みがない）

Q6.　Working as vloggers sounds really good because they can work freely and have fun all the time.

Q7.　working / vlogger

Q8.　1

Q9.　2

Q10.　3

解説

Q1.　問題は「著者が子どもだった時、何になりたいと思っていたでしょう？」という意味。最初の段落の序盤に、What did you want to be when you were little?（あなたは小さかった時、何になりたかったですか？）と質問を投げかけ、少し後に I wanted to be a singer（私は歌手になりたかったです）と答えている。また、その後に、I saw many idols on TV, and I wanted to be like them.（テレビでたくさんのアイドルを見て、彼女ら〈彼ら〉のようになりたいと思っていました）と書かれているため、idol も正解。

Q2.　問題は「著者は大学にいた時、何を学んだでしょう？」という意味。最初の段落の終盤に、I studied journalism in college and got a job as a journalist after I graduated.（私はジャーナリズムを大学で学び、大学卒業後はジ

ャーナリストとして仕事を得ました）と書かれている。

Q3.　1. は、2段落目の序盤に、some surveys done in Japan in 2018 show that many children want to be vloggers when they grow up（2018年に日本で行われたいくつかの調査によると、多くの子どもたちは大きくなったらビデオブロガーになりたいと思っています）と書かれているので◯。

　　2. は、2段落目の中盤に、some companies will ask you to advertise their products, so you will be able to get money by using their products in your videos.（一部の会社は彼らの商品を宣伝してほしいとあなたに頼むでしょうから、あなたの動画で彼らの商品を使うことでお金を得ることができるようになります）と書かれており「企業が自分にお金を払う」形なので×。

　　3. は、3段落目の序盤にビデオブロガーについて、It sounds like a great job, but why are some parents against it?（素晴らしい仕事のように聞こえますが、なぜ一部の親は反対なのか？）と書かれているので◯。

　　4. は、2段落目の終盤に、Some successful vloggers make 100 million yen or more every year.（一部の成功しているビデオブロガーは、毎年1億円以上稼いでいます）と書かれているので×。

Q4.　2段落目の終盤に、A YouTuber is another name for a vlogger（ユーチューバーは、ビデオブロガーの別の名前です）と書かれている。

Q5.　3段落目に、many vloggers cannot make enough money to live.（多くのビデオブロガーは生活するための十分なお金を得られていません）、because vloggers may have to live poorly until they become famous.（おそらくビデオブロガーは、有名になるまで貧しく生活しないといけないからです）と書かれている。また、You need to be creative, too, because 〜 so people will want to see your videos.（あなたは、創造的である必要もあります。なぜなら〜人々はあなたの動画を見た

いと思うでしょう）とも書かれている。そして、vloggers need to film themselves, edit their videos, and upload them by themselves, and they need to do this every day!（ビデオブロガーは、自分自身を撮影し、動画を編集、そしてそれらをアップロードするのを自分自身で行い、これを毎日する必要があります）、They do not have summer or winter vacations.（彼らには夏休みや冬休みはありません）と書かれている。

Q6. 下線部（2）のthatが含まれる、Is that true?（それは本当でしょうか？）の前の文で、Some children think that working as a vlogger sounds really good because they can work freely and have fun all the time.（一部の子どもたちは、ビデオブロガーとして働くのは本当に良さそう〈良く聞こえる〉と考えています。なぜなら、いつも自由に働け、楽しめるからです）と書かれており、後の文で、The answer is "No." Children should know working as a vlogger is hard（答えは「いいえ」です。子どもたちはビデオブロガーとして働くのは大変だということを知っておくべきです）と書かれているため、thatが指しているのは「一部の子どもたちが考えている内容」だということが分かる（「一部の子どもたちがビデオブロガーは良い仕事だと考えているという事実」ではない）。

Q7. 下線部（3）の the difficultiesは、4段落目の序盤に登場する、Children should know working as a vlogger is hard（子どもたちはビデオブロガーとして働くのは大変だということを知っておくべきです）の内容を指しているため、「ビデオブロガーとして働く大変さ」となる。前置詞（of）の後にはto不定詞は使えず動名詞が使われるため、最初のカッコにはworkingが入る。

Q8. 下線部（4）のgo for it が登場する文が、If one of my friends tells me that he or she wants to be a vlogger, I will say go for it because some vloggers are very successful and rich, and he or she may become one of them.（も

し私の友人の一人がビデオブロガーになりたいと言ったら、私は go for it と言うでしょう。なぜなら、一部のビデオブロガーは大きな成功を収めていてお金持ちであり、彼らの一員になれるかもしれないからです）となっていることから「頑張ってみなよ」という意味だと分かる。

Q9. 選択肢の意味は
1. I will be able to help her.（私は彼女を助けられるでしょう）
2. I will tell her to answer my questions first.（最初に私の質問に答えてと彼女に言うでしょう）
3. I will not be happy about it.（私はそれについてうれしくは思わないでしょう）
4. she will have to buy a new video camera.（彼女は新しいビデオカメラを買わないといけないでしょう）
（ア）が登場する前後で、If my daughter tells me she wants to be a vlogger,（ア）"Are you ～? You may be ～. Do you really think you will be OK?"（もし私の娘がビデオブロガーになりたいと言ったら（ア）「あなたは～？　あなたは～かもしれないよ。あなたは大丈夫だろうと本当に思う？」）と質問をしていることから、（ア）に入るのは2.となる。

Q10. 3.は、最後の段落の中盤に、If my daughter tells me she wants to be a vlogger（もし私の娘がビデオブロガーになりたいと言ったら）と「実際の話」ではなく「仮定の話」が書かれているので、本文の内容とは異なる。
1.は、最初の段落の中盤に、I joined a dance team to practice dancing, too.（私はダンスを練習するためにダンスチームにも入りました）と書かれているので本文の内容と合っている。
2.は、4段落の終盤に、Many high school students answered that they wanted to become teachers, computer programmers, or engineers instead.（その代わり、多くの高校生は、教員、プログラマー、エンジニアになりたいと答えています）と書かれているので本文の内容と合っている。

4. は、3段落目の終盤に、many famous vloggers in Japan upload 400 or more videos every year.（日本にいる多くの有名なビデオブロガーは毎年400本以上の動画をアップロードしています）と書かれているので本文の内容と合っている。

全文和訳例

1. あなたはビデオブロガーになりたいですか？

2. あなたは小さかった時、何になりたかったですか？

3. プロ野球選手になりたかったですか？ それとも、医者になりたかったですか？

4. 私は歌手になりたかったです。なぜなら、私は人々の前で歌うのが好きだったからです。

5. 私が小学校にいた時は、テレビでたくさんのアイドルを見て、彼女ら（彼ら）のようになりたいと思っていました。

6. 私は妹（姉）と歌を練習するためにカラオケに行きました。

7. 私はダンスを練習するためにダンスチームにも入りました。

8. 一生懸命努力したと思うのですが、人気のある歌手になるのは本当に難しいということに気づいたので、他の何かになろうと決めました。

9. しかし、私の質問は「私は何になりたいの？」でした。

10. 私は高校にいた際、書くことが好きでした。

11. 実際、私はブログのサイトを持っており、記事を書くのを楽しんでいました。そのため、私は大きくなったらジャーナリストになろうと決めました。

12. 私はジャーナリズムを大学で学び、大学卒業後はジャーナリストとして仕事を得ました。

13. 私はジャーナリストになれてうれしく思っています。なぜなら、記事を書くのは楽しいからです。

14. 私が言いたいことは何か？

15. 子どもたちの夢は成長するにつれて変わるかも知れないということを言いたいのです。

16. なぜ私はこのことを言っているのか？

17. 私がこのことを言っている理由は、2018年に日本で行われたいくつかの調査によると、多くの子どもたちは大きくなったらビデオブロガーになりたいと思っています。そして、一部の親はそれがいい考えだとは思っていないからです。

18. ビデオブロガーとは誰か？

19. ビデオブロガーとは、ブロガー（ブログを書くことでお金を得ている人たち）のような人たちですが、ビデオブロガーは動画を使います。

20. 彼らは自分自身を撮影し、世界中の人たちに見せるためにウェブサイトに彼らの動画をアップロードします。

21. もしたくさんの人たちが彼らの動画を見たら、ウェブサイトからお金がもらえます。

22. もし、あなたが有名なビデオブロガーになったら、一部の会社は彼らの商品を宣伝してほしいとあなたに頼むでしょうから、あなたの動画で彼らの商品を使うことでお金を得ることができるようになります。

23. ユーチューバーは、ビデオブロガーの別の名前です。なぜなら、たくさんのビデオブロガーは、彼らの動画をユーチューブ（彼らの動画を共有できる人気のウェブサイト）にアップロードするからです。

24. 一部の成功しているビデオブロガーは、毎年1億円以上稼いでいます。

25. 彼らは良い家に住み、カッコいい車を運転し、良い食べ物を食べます。

26. 素晴らしい仕事のように聞こえますが、なぜ一部の親は反対なのか？

27. 彼らが反対している理由はビデオブロガーとして生きていくことは簡単ではないと考えているからです。

28. 彼らは、ただ誰でもできるとは考えていません。

29. 実際、多くのビデオブロガーは生活するための十分なお金を得られていません。

30. 彼らは別の仕事を持っています。なぜなら、ウェブサイトからは一切お金をもらっていないため、ただ彼ら自身の動画を作るだけでは生

活できないのです。

31. 一部の人たちは、成功したビデオブロガーになるのは成功した俳優になるようなものと言います。なぜなら、おそらくビデオブロガーは、有名になるまで貧しく生活しないといけないからです。

32. あなたは、創造的である必要もあります。なぜなら、あなたは興味深い、面白い、あるいはユニークな動画を作る必要があるからです。そうすれば、人々はあなたの動画を見たいと思うでしょう。

33. もし、あなたの動画が良くなければ、誰も見ないので、あなたはお金を全く得られないということを意味します。

34. 更に、ビデオブロガーは、自分自身を撮影し、動画を編集、そしてそれらをアップロードするのを自分自身で行い、これを毎日する必要があります。

35. 実際、日本にいる多くの有名なビデオブロガーは毎年400本以上の動画をアップロードしています。

36. それは毎日1本以上の動画を作っているということを意味します。

37. 彼らには夏休みや冬休みはありません。

38. 彼らは人々が休んでいる時に、一生懸命働かないといけないのです。

39. 彼らの仕事が楽しくなければ、それはとても難しいことになるでしょう。

40. 一部の子どもたちは、ビデオブロガーとして働くのは本当に良さそう（良く聞こえる）と考えています。なぜなら、いつも自由に働け、楽しめるからです。

41. それは本当でしょうか？　答えは「いいえ」です。

42. 子どもたちはビデオブロガーとして働くのは大変だということを知っておくべきです。しかし、子どもたちはそれをビデオブロガーの動画からは理解することができません。そのため、一部の親は心配しているのです。

43. しかし、それは大きな問題ではありません。なぜなら、子どもたちは成長すれば、その大変さを理解するからです。

44. 実際、日本で行われた他の調査によると多くの高校生はビデオブロガーになるのは現実的ではないと思っています。

45. その代わり、多くの高校生は、教員、プログラマー、エンジニアになりたいと答えています。

46. 私は、ビデオブロガーになることは悪い考えだとは言っていませんが、ユニークな仕事ではあります。

47. もしあなたが、自分を撮影し、動画を編集し、世界に見せるのが好きなのであれば、ビデオブロガーになるのは素晴らしい考えだと思います。

48. もし私の友人の一人がビデオブロガーになりたいと言ったら、私は、頑張ってみなよと言うでしょう。なぜなら、一部のビデオブロガーは大きな成功を収めていてお金持ちであり、彼らの一員になれるかもしれないからです。

49. もし私の娘がビデオブロガーになりたいと言ったら、最初に私の質問に答えてと彼女に言うでしょう。

50. 「あなたは、これができると本当に確信している？　あなたはとても貧しいかもしれない。

51. 休日もないかもしれないよ。あなたは大丈夫だろうと本当に思う？」

52. もし彼女がこれらの質問に「はい」と答えたら、私は彼女をサポートするだろうと思います。

4 文の真ん中に足される副詞

(p.60)

解答例

Q1. (a) 1 (b) 3 (c) 2 (d) 2 (e) 1

Q2. 3

Q3. her grandparents

Q4. Because he lived in Canada for two years when he was in elementary school.

Q5. 4

Q6. 2

Q7. NZ Reports

Q8. 1

Q9. 3

Q10. 4

解説

Q1. (a) 一般動詞の文にalmost（副詞）を入れる場合、一般動詞の前に足される。

(b) 助動詞の文にnever（副詞）を入れる場合は、助動詞の後に足される。

(c) be動詞の文にalready（副詞）を入れる場合は、be動詞の後に足される。

(d) be動詞の文にactually（副詞）を入れる場合は、be動詞の後に足される。

(e) be動詞の文にalways（副詞）を入れる場合は、be動詞の後に足される。

Q2. 2段落目の中盤に、she was born and grew up in New Zealand, ～ so Rachel never had to learn Japanese when she was in New Zealand（彼女はニュージーランドで生まれ育ったので、～ レイチェルはニュージーランドにいる時は日本語を全く学ばないでよかったのです）と書かれている。

1.は、2段落目の序盤に、her first language is English（彼女の第一言語が英語だからです）と書かれている。

2.は、2段落目の中盤に、she always wanted to go to Japan and learn about their culture（彼女は日本に行き、日本の〈彼らの〉文化について学びたいといつも思っていました）と書かれている。

4.は、2段落目の序盤に、her mother is Japanese（彼女のお母さんは日本人）と書かれている。

Q3. 問題は「レイチェルは日本に引っ越してきました。彼女は誰と一緒に住んでいるでしょう?」という意味。

2段落目の序盤に、she is living with her grandparents now.（現在、彼女は彼女の祖父母と一緒に住んでいます）と書かれている。

Q4. 問題は「フミヤは英語が上手です（フミヤの英語は良いです）。なぜでしょう?」という意味。

3段落目の序盤にフミヤについて、He can speak English well because he lived in Canada for two years when he was in elementary school.（彼は英語を上手に話すことができます。なぜなら、彼は小学校にいた時に2年間カナダに住んでいたからです）と書かれている。

Q5. economistは、economyという単語に関連していることは推測できる（art →artistのように）。economyという単語は、4段落の序盤で、Our economy is not very good now.（我々のeconomyは、現在あまり良くないから）という文が登場し、続く文で、many people are poor because they cannot find jobs（たくさんの人が貧しい思いをしているんだよ。〈なぜなら〉彼らは仕事を見つけることができないから）とあることから、economyは、お金・経済に関わる単語だということが推測できる。そのため、答えは経済学者となる。

Q6. 下線部（2）の、pulled out her smartphone.は「彼女のスマートフォンを取り出しました」という意味。下線部（2）の直後に、I always use this website to read news from New Zealand.（ニュージーランドのニュースを読むのにいつも私はこのウェブサイトを使っているんだ）と書かれているため、レイチェルはウェブサイトを紹介するためにスマートフォンを取り出したことが分かる。

Q7. 下線部（3）の、wrote the name.は「その名前を書きました」という意味。下線部（3）の

直前のやりとりでフミヤが、What is the name of the website?（ウェブサイトの名前は何なの？）とたずねたのに対しレイチェルが、it is NZ Reports.（NZ Reportsだよ）と答え、フミヤが、Alright. I will take a look at it.（なるほど。見てみるよ）と答えているため、書いた名前は NZ Reports と分かる。

Q8. 下線部 (4) のthatが含まれる文は、I like to read in a quiet place and our classroom is a perfect place for that,（僕は本を静かな場所で読むのが好きで、僕たちの教室は〈それをするためには〉完璧な場所なんだ）となっているため、thatが指すのは「静かなところで本を読むこと」だと分かる。

Q9. 下線部 (5) の the viewは「（その）景色」という意味。下線部 (5) の直後にフミヤが、There aren't any tall buildings, so you can clearly see the sunset from here if the weather is nice.（高い建物が全くないから、天気が良ければ夕日がここからはっきり見えるんだ）と発言している。

Q10. 最後の段落の終盤にフミヤが教室からの景色について、I think it is pretty rare in Tokyo.（東京ではけっこう珍しいと思う）と発言していることから、フミヤとレイチェルが通っている学校は東京にあることが分かるため、正解は4.となる。
1.は、2段落目の序盤にレイチェルの日本語力に関して、Her Japanese language skills are still low（彼女の日本語力はまだ低いです）と書かれている。
2.は、3段落目の終盤に、he does not want to speak English with her every day（彼は、毎日彼女と英語で話したいとは思っていません）と書かれている。
3.は、4段落目の序盤にフミヤが読んでいる本について、This book is about the Japanese economy. Our economy is not very good now. ～. so I want to know why.（この本は日本の経済についてだよ。我々の経済は、現在あまり良くないから。～。だから、なぜなのかを知りたくてね）と答えている。

1. 「なんでまだ教室にいるの、フミヤ？」レイチェルは後ろから彼にたずねました。

2. フミヤは驚きました。なぜなら、彼しか教室にいないと思ったからです。

3. 「わぁ、何で脅かすんだよ（何でそんなことをしたんだ）？ （僕の）椅子から落ちるところだったじゃん」フミヤはたずねました。

4. 「あぁ、ごめん。面白いかと思ったけど、そうじゃなかったみたいね。ごめん。

5. もう二度としないから」彼女はほぼ笑みながら答えたので、そんなに本気ではないということをフミヤは分かっていました。

6. 「それで、何をしているの？ 宿題をしているの？」彼女はたずねました。

7. 「いいや。それは終わっているんだ。実は本を読んでいたんだよ」フミヤは答えました。

8. 「どんな種類の本なの？」レイチェルはたずねました。

9. 「おやおや。まただ。今回は何と彼女に言おう」フミヤは思いました。

10. 彼女がその質問をするだろうということを彼は分かっていました。なぜなら、彼女はいつも興味津々だからです。

11. 彼らが日本のドラマを一緒に見ていた時、ドラマの1つ1つの会話すべてをフミヤは訳さないといけませんでした。なぜなら、彼女は全てを知りたがったからです。

12. 彼は「やりたくない」とは言えません。なぜなら、初めて彼らが出会った時、彼は「もし何か必要なことがあれば、僕がいつでも助けるよ」と彼女に伝えていたからです。しかし、今彼はそれを少し後悔しています。

13. レイチェルはニュージーランドから来た生徒で2週間前にフミヤの高校に来ました。

14. 実は、彼女のお母さんは日本人で、現在、彼女は彼女の祖父母と一緒に住んでいます。

15. 彼女の日本語力はどうなのか？

16. 彼女の日本語力は、まだ低いです。なぜなら、彼女はニュージーランドで生まれ育ったので、彼女の第一言語が英語だからです。

17. 更に、彼女のお母さんはとても上手に英語を

15

話すことができるので、レイチェルはニュージーランドにいる時は日本語を全く学ばないでよかったのです。

18. しかし、彼女は日本に行き、日本の（彼らの）文化について学びたいといつも思っていました。なぜなら、彼女は自分の背景に興味を持っていたからです。

19. 彼女は更に留学にも興味を持っていました。なぜなら、彼女の先生の一人が「留学したことを絶対に後悔しない」とよく言っていたからです。そのため、彼女は日本に1年住み、そこで高校に行くことを決めました。

20. 彼女は、日本語の読み書きを練習するためいくつかの授業を取りました。

21. 彼女は更に日本語の話すことと聞くことを彼女のお母さんと練習しました。

22. 彼女たちは、レイチェルの日本にいる祖父母についてよく話しました。なぜなら、彼女は彼らと住む予定だったからです。

23. レイチェルは、フミヤのことを気に入っています。なぜなら、彼は彼女に対して優しいからです。

24. 彼らが初めて出会った時、彼女は、彼の英語に驚きました。なぜなら、彼は英語をとても上手に話せたからです（彼の英語はとても良かったからです）。

25. なぜ彼はそんなにも上手に英語が話せるのでしょう？

26. 彼は英語を上手に話すことができます。なぜなら、彼は小学校にいた時に2年間カナダに住んでいたからです。

27. レイチェルは時々英語を話すのを恋しく思うので、彼女は彼と話すことを本当に楽しんでいます。

28. フミヤもレイチェルと話すのが好きなのでしょうか？　はい、そうです。

29. 彼も好きです。なぜなら、彼女と英語を話す練習が（彼は）できるからです。

30. しかし、彼は、毎日彼女と英語で話したいとは思っていません。なぜなら、彼女はたいていたくさんの質問をするので、彼はとても疲れてしまうからです。

31. 「あぁ、この本？　この本は日本の経済についてだよ。

32. 我々の経済は、現在あまり良くないから。

33. 実際、たくさんの人が貧しい思いをしているんだよ。（なぜなら）彼らは仕事を見つけることができないから。だから、なぜなのかを知りたくてね。

34. ニュージーランドの経済は良いの？」フミヤはたずねました。

35. 「大丈夫だと思うよ。

36. とても良いというわけではないけど、ひどいとも思わないし」レイチェルは答えました。

37. 「だけど、私はプロの経済学者じゃないから、本当に定かではないかな。

38. もし、ニュージーランドの経済に興味があるのなら、このウェブサイトを見てみるべきだよ」レイチェルは、彼女のスマートフォンを取り出しました。

39. 「これ。ニュージーランドのニュースを読むのにいつも私はこのウェブサイトを使っているんだ。

40. あぁ、このウェブサイトも確認してみるべきだよ。

41. とても便利なんだ。なぜなら、実際にニュージーランドの（彼らの）ニュース番組を見ることができるから」

42. フミヤはスクリーンをのぞき込み、たずねました。「ウェブサイトの名前は何なの？」

43. 「あぁ、NZレポートだよ。けっこう簡単に見つけられると思うよ」レイチェルは答えました。

44. 「なるほど。見てみるよ。ありがとう」フミヤはノートを取り出し、その名前を書きました。

45. 「どういたしまして。あなたは放課後にいつも教室に残っているの？」レイチェルはたずねました。

46. 「えっと、いつもではないかな。だけど、時々だね。なぜなら、僕は本を静かな場所で読むのが好きで、僕たちの教室は（それをするためには）完璧な場所なんだ」彼は窓の外を見て、続けました

47. 「僕は、ここからの景色も好きでね。

48. 高い建物が全くないから、天気が良ければ夕日がここからはっきり見えるんだ。

49. 東京ではけっこう珍しいと思う。

50. 葉っぱが色を変えるから、この季節の間は特にきれいだよ」

51. レイチェルも窓の外を見ました。

52. 「今日は夕日が見られると思う?」彼女がたずねました。

53. 「そう思うよ。もうすぐ4時だから、もしあと30分待てるのであれば、見られると思うよ」

54. レイチェルは彼女の腕時計に目をやり、時間を確認しました。

55. 彼女は、彼女のバスを逃したくありませんでした。なぜなら、もし彼女(の帰り)が遅れると、彼女の祖父母が(彼女のことを)心配するからです。

56. 彼女は再び彼女の腕時計を確認しました。「十分な時間があると思うかな」彼女は思いました。

57. 「オーケー。待つよ。きれいだといいな(良いことを望むよ)」レイチェルは言いました。

58. 「信じて。素晴らしいから」フミヤは答えました。

---

5 英語の文型

(p.76)

解答例

Q1. 2

Q2. 大学生の親

Q3. six

Q4. 4

Q5. they always make me happy

Q6. 3

Q7. 4

Q8. final exams

Q9. 必要な情報は携帯電話で調べることができ、英語の看板がいたるところにあるから。

Q10. 1

解説

Q1. I need to pay my college expenses.(僕は僕のcollege expensesを払う必要があるから)という内容から、college expensesはヘンリーが払うものだということが分かる。また、次のカオリの発言で、they usually pay their own college expenses, such as their tuition and textbooks.(彼らはたいてい自分自身で授業料や教科書といったcollege expensesを払っているから)と書かれていることから、大学生活でかかる費用だということが分かる。

Q2. 本文序盤、大学で勉強するのに必要な費用について話をしている際、カオリが、It is different from many college students in Japan because they don't usually pay their own college expenses.(それは日本の多くの大学生とは違うね。なぜなら、彼らはたいてい自分自身では大学生活でかかる費用を払っていないから)と発言し、その直後にヘンリーがWho does then?(それじゃあ、誰が払っているの?)と質問したのに対し、カオリがTheir parents do.(彼らの〈両〉親だよ)と答えている。

Q3. (ア)の直前でカオリが、How many students do you teach?(何人の生徒を教えているの?)と具体的な生徒の数をたずねており、直後

に、You teach many students.（たくさんの生徒を教えているんだね）と発言しているためmanyを入れるのは不自然。（ア）の直後にヘンリーが、I teach three elementary school students, one junior high school student, and two high school students.（3人の小学生、1人の中学生、そして2人の高校生を教えているんだ）と発言していることから、生徒は6人いることが分かる。

Q4. 下線部（2）の直前で、Wow! You teach many students.（わぁ！　たくさんの生徒を教えているんだね）と発言していることから、No wonder you are busy.は「忙しいわけだ」という意味になることが推測できる。

Q5. make A B＝AをBにする（SVOCの形）
一般動詞の文にalways（副詞）を入れる場合、一般動詞の前に足される。

Q6. 本文中盤でヘンリーが、Most of my students are Japanese.（僕の生徒のほとんどは日本人なんだよ）と発言していることから全員が日本人ではないということが分かるため、答えは3.となる。
1.は、本文中盤でカオリがヘンリーに、You teach many students.（たくさんの生徒を教えているんだね）と発言している。
2.は、本文序盤でヘンリーが、I live alone（僕は一人で住んでいるんだ）と発言している。
4.は、本文中盤でヘンリーが、I teach them many subjects. For example, Math, Science, Social Studies, and English.（僕はたくさんの科目を教えているよ。例えば、数学、科学、社会科、そして英語）と発言している。

Q7. 下線部（4）の直前でヘンリーが、one of my American students says he wants to go to college in Japan, so I teach him Japanese. Actually, we are planning to visit Japan this summer.（僕のアメリカ人の生徒の1人は日本の大学に行きたいと言っているから、日本語を教えていてね。実は、この夏に僕たちは日本を訪ねる計画を立てているんだ）と話しており、下線部（4）の直後にカオリが、I live in Tochigi, so if you are going to stay in the

Kanto area, I think I can.（私は栃木に住んでいるから、関東地方に滞在するのであればできると思うよ）と言っていることから、Do you think you can show us around?は「案内してもらうことは可能かな？」という意味になることが分かる。

Q8. 本文終盤でカオリが、I will have my final exams in the last week of July,（期末試験が7月の最終週にある予定）と発言している。

Q9. 本文終盤でカオリが、I don't think you will need any help in Tokyo if you have a cell phone because you can always use your cell phone if you need to find something, and you will see English signs everywhere,（携帯電話を持っていれば東京では全く助けが必要にならないと思うよ。なぜなら、何か見つけたい場合はいつでも携帯電話を使うことができるし、英語の看板をいたるところで目にするだろうから）と発言している。

Q10. 本文終盤でヘンリーは、We are planning to go to Nikko Toshogu Shrine, so we can see you when we visit there.（僕たちは、日光東照宮に行く計画を立てているから、僕たちがそこを訪ねる時に会えるね）と発言しているが、日本に到着して最初に行くとは言っていないため、答えは1.となる。
2.は、本文序盤で大学にかかる費用について話している際ヘンリーが、In America, some people work full-time for a few years before they start going to college because they think they will not be able to study and work part-time at the same time.（アメリカでは、大学に行き始める前に数年正社員として働く人もいくらかいるんだ。なぜなら、彼らは勉強とアルバイトを同時にできないだろうと考えているから）と発言している。
3.は、本文終盤でカオリが、I have some friends in Tokyo, and ～（私には東京に何人か友だちがいて、～）と発言している。
4.は、本文中盤でヘンリーが教えている生徒たちについて話をしている際、I enjoy teaching them（彼らを教えるのは楽しいよ）

と発言している。

（カオリがインターネットでヘンリーと話している）

1. カオリ：こんにちは、ヘンリー。どうしている？

2. ヘンリー：やあ、カオリ。元気だよ。少し疲れているけど、問題ではないかな。

3. カオリ：何で疲れているの？

4. ヘンリー：（なぜなら）今日働かないといけなくて、さっき終わったからだよ。

5. 3時間休憩を取らずに働くのは本当に大変だったよ。

6. カオリ：まぁ、アルバイトをしているなんて知らなかったよ。何をしているの？

7. ヘンリー：家庭教師として働いているんだ。今日は3人の子どもたちを教えなくちゃいけなかったんだよ。

8. カオリ：どれくらいの頻度で働いているの？

9. ヘンリー：ほぼ毎日だね。（なぜなら）僕は、僕の大学生活でかかる費用を払う必要があるから。

10. カオリ：なるほど。アメリカの大学生の多くはアルバイトをしないといけないって聞いているよ。なぜなら、彼らはたいてい自分自身で授業料や教科書といった大学生活でかかる費用を払っているから。

11. ヘンリー：そうだね。更に、僕は一人で住んでいるんだ。だから、僕は僕の生活費も払わないといけない。

12. そして、何だと思う？ それは珍しいことではないんだ。

13. カオリ：わぁ。それは日本の多くの大学生とは違うね。なぜなら、彼らはたいてい自分自身では大学生活でかかる費用を払っていないから。

14. ヘンリー：それじゃあ、誰が払っているの？

15. カオリ：彼らの（両）親だよ。

16. 更に、彼らが（彼らの）家族から離れて住む場合は、たいてい彼らの（両）親が彼らの生活費を払い、いくらかの仕送りも彼らに渡している

17. るかな。だから、多くの学生は全く働く必要がないんだよ。

18. ヘンリー：彼らはラッキーだね。（なぜなら）お金の心配をしなくていいんだもん。

19. アメリカでは、大学に行き始める前に数年正社員として働く人もいくらかいるんだ。なぜなら、彼らは勉強とアルバイトを同時にできないだろうと考えているから。

20. カオリ：それは、興味深いね。何人の生徒を教えているの？

21. ヘンリー：6人の生徒を教えているんだ。

22. カオリ：わぁ！ たくさんの生徒を教えているんだね。忙しいわけだ。

23. ヘンリー：そうだね。3人の小学生、1人の中学生、そして2人の高校生を教えているんだ。

24. 大変だけど、彼らを教えるのは楽しいよ（僕は、彼らを教えるのを楽しんでいるよ）。なぜなら、彼らはとてもいい生徒たちだからね。

25. 何人かの生徒は手紙を書いてくれて、それらを読むのは本当に楽しいんだ。

26. たとえ、僕の気分がすぐれない時でも、（それらは）いつも僕を幸せな気持ちにしてくれるんだ。

27. 僕の生徒の1人は7歳で、彼女は僕のことをヘンヘンと呼ぶんだ。（なぜなら）彼女はヘンリーと言えないから。

28. （彼女は）とてもかわいいよ。

29. カオリ：なるほど。何を彼らに教えているの？

30. ヘンリー：僕はたくさんの科目を教えているよ。

31. 例えば、数学、科学、社会科、そして英語。

32. カオリ：英語も教えているの？

33. ヘンリー：あぁ、言うのを忘れていた。僕の生徒のほとんどは日本人なんだよ。

34. 彼らは、彼らのお父さんの仕事が理由でアメリカに来ているんだ。

35. 彼らの一部は、少ししか英語が話せないから、彼らには英語を教えているんだよ。

36. 僕は少し日本語が話せるから、僕らはたいてい日本語で話すんだ。

37. 大学で日本語の授業をいくつか取っておいて良かったよ。

37. カオリ：なるほどね。

38. ヘンリー：あぁ、そういえば、僕のアメリカ人の生徒の1人は日本の大学に行きたいと言っているから、日本語を教えていてね。

39. 実は、この夏に僕たちは日本を訪ねる計画を立てているんだ。

40. 案内してもらうことは可能かな？

41. カオリ：えっと、私は栃木に住んでいるから、関東地方に滞在するのであればできると思うよ。

42. ヘンリー：僕たちは、宮城、東京、京都といったたくさんの場所を訪ねる予定だから、関東地方に滞在するとは思わないかな。

43. あぁ、そうだ（分かった）。

44. 僕たちは、日光東照宮に行く計画を立てているから、僕たちがそこを訪ねる時に会えるね。

45. カオリ：それは良いね。

46. 私は日光で育ったから、その地域周辺にある良い場所をいくつか紹介するよ。

47. いつ日本に来る予定なの？

48. ヘンリー：7月に訪ねる予定だね。後でスケジュールを送るよ。

49. カオリ：オーケー。言わなくちゃいけないことがあって。

50. 期末試験が7月の最終週にある予定だから、その週か、その前の週に栃木に来る場合は、あなたたちに会えないだろうから。

51. ヘンリー：分かったよ。

52. カオリ：どれくらいの間、日本に滞在する予定なの？

53. ヘンリー：おそらく、数日しか滞在しないと思うよ。（なぜなら）僕たちは、たくさんお金を持っていないから。

54. 僕らはヒッチハイクするつもりなんだ。（なぜなら）交通費にたくさんのお金を使いたくないから。

55. カオリ：良い考えだね。

56. 電車やバスを使うと、けっこう高くなるだろうからね。だけど、夜行バスはそんなに悪くないって聞いたよ。

57. 一部の旅行者は夜行バスを使うって。なぜなら、バスで寝ることができるから、ホテル代

を払う心配もないからね。

58. インターネットで確認して、いくらか情報を得る（見つける）べきだよ。

59. ヘンリー：オーケー。そうするよ。

60. カオリ：あぁ、もう1つ。私には東京に何人か友だちがいて、彼らは英語が話せるんだ。

61. 彼らのうちの何人かは、あなたたちを助けることができるかもしれないから、彼らに聞いてみるね。

62. だけど、実を言うと、携帯電話を持っていれば東京では全く助けが必要にならないと思うよ。なぜなら、何か見つけたい場合はいつでも携帯電話を使うことができるし、英語の看板をいたるところで目にするだろうから。だから、あなたの携帯電話の充電器を持ってくるのだけは忘れないでね。

63. ヘンリー：ははは。オーケー。覚えておくよ。

6 比較級

(p.94)

解答例

Q1.　2

Q2.　(a) 3　(b) 1

Q3.　次のうちの2つ。

・高校にいた時、好きな科目が生物学だったから。

・高校にいた時、生物学は他の科学の授業より簡単だと思ったから。

・生物学の成績は、化学や物理の授業の成績より良かったから。

Q4.　1年半

Q5.　4

Q6.　4

Q7.　3

Q8.　1

Q9.　more / expensive / than

Q10.　2

解説

Q1.　2.は、1段落目の終盤で教室を間違えた生徒に対し、Your classroom is 219, so 〜（あなたの教室は219なので、〜）と説明していることから、全ての授業が209で行われているわけではないことが分かるため、正解は2.となる。

1.は、1段落目の序盤で、We have three Biology teachers, and 〜（〈我々には〉3人の生物学の先生がいて、〜）と説明している。

3.は、1段落目の中盤で教室を間違えた生徒に対し、Who is your teacher? Ms. Conner?（先生は誰ですか？　コナー先生？）と聞いている。

4.は、2段落目の序盤で、I grew up in a small town in California.（私はカリフォルニアの小さな町で育ちました）と説明している。

Q2.　比較級の基本の形は "形容詞er + than + 比べるもの""副詞er + than + 比べるもの"。つづりが長い形容詞 / 副詞の場合は "more形容詞 + than + 比べるもの""more 副詞 +

than + 比べるもの" となる（比べるものが明白な場合は「than + 比べるもの」が省略される場合もある）。

(a) と (b) が入る文は「私たちの湖は、タッパン湖よりも大きくはありませんでしたが、より美しかったと思います」という意味。

(a) で登場するbigは "bigger than 比べるもの" となるため、3.が正解となる。

(b) で登場するbeautifulは "more beautiful"（than + 比べるものが省略された形）となるため、1.が正解となる。

Q3.　2段落目の中盤に、so I decided to study Biology in college.（そのため、私は大学で生物学を学ぶことにしました）と書かれており、その前に、When I was in high school, my favorite subject was Biology.（私が高校にいた時は、私の好きな科目は生物学でした）、I thought it was easier than other Science classes.（他の科学の授業よりも簡単だと思っていました）、In fact, my final grade in Biology was better than my final grades in Chemistry or Physics,（実際、私の生物学の最終成績は化学や物理学の最終成績よりも良かったです）と答えとなる3つのことが書かれている。

Q4.　2段落目の終盤に、It took five years for me to graduate from college,（私は、大学を卒業するのに5年間かかりました）と書かれており、3段落目の序盤にウィルソン先生の双子のお姉さん（妹さん）について書かれており、it took only three and a half years for her to graduate.（彼女は卒業するのに3年半しかかかりませんでした）と書かれているため、差は1年半となる。

Q5.　下線部 (1) の syllabus が含まれる文章で、I will pass out the syllabus, so you can see my email address, the goals of this class, the class schedule, and so on.（シラバスを配りますので、私のメールアドレス、この授業のゴール、授業のスケジュールなどが分かるでしょう）と書かれている。

Q6.　下線部 (2) は「生物学とは何でしょう？　何

をこの授業で我々は学ぶでしょう?」という意味。下線部 (2) の直前に、If you know the answer, please raise your hand. Ready? (もし答えを知っている場合は、手を挙げてください。いいですか?)、そして下線部 (2) の直後に、Does anyone know the answer? Nobody? That's fine. (誰か答えを知っていますか? 誰も知らないのですか? いいでしょう) と書かれているため、誰も手を挙げなかったのが分かる。

Q7. 下線部 (3) は「これらの2つの写真を見てください」という意味。下線部 (3) の直後で、Which one is a real duck? (どちらが本物のアヒルでしょう?) と質問し、生徒たちが答えた後に、How did you know? What are the differences? Can anyone answer? (どうして分かったのですか? 違いは何ですか? 誰か答えられますか?) と質問し、最後から2番目の段落の最初で、So, the meaning of the word "life" is very difficult to understand. (このように、「命」という言葉の意味を理解するのはとても難しいのです) と説明していることから、3. が答えだということが分かる。

Q8. 1. は「(あなたたちが) 次の授業に行く」という意味。
2. は「(あなたたちが) あなたたちのシラバスを確認する」という意味。
3. は「(あなたたちが) 他の科学の授業を取る」という意味。
4. は「(あなたたちが) 走りに行く」という意味。
下線部 (4) の直前に、We are running out of time. (時間がなくなってきています) と説明しており、本文の最後で、Okay, that's all for today. I'll see you tomorrow. (オーケー。今日の分は、これで全てです。また明日会いましょう) と説明していることから、生物学の授業が終わり、生徒たちが次の授業に行く直前だということが分かる。

Q9. 下線部 (5) は「スーパーマートの (彼らの) エプロンは、(彼らの) ポテトチップスよりも安いと思います」という意味。答える文は主語

が「スーパーマートの (彼らの) ポテトチップス」となっているので「スーパーマートの (彼らの) ポテトチップスは、(彼らの) エプロンよりも高いと思います」という文を作る必要があるため、( ) には、more expensive than が入る (expensive は、つづりが長いので expensiver にはならない)。

Q10. 2. は「生徒たちは安いエプロンをスーパーマートで買うことができる」という意味。最後の段落の中盤で、We will have the first experiment next week, so please bring an apron. If you don't have one, go to Super Mart and get one. They have cheap aprons. (私たちは最初の実験を来週行いますので、エプロンを持ってきてください。もし持っていない場合は、スーパーマートに行って1つ買って〈手に入れて〉ください。〈彼らは〉安いエプロンを売っています〈持っています〉から) と書かれているので正解。
1. は「ウィルソン先生は化学を教えている」という意味。本文の最初に、Welcome to Biology. I am Ben Wilson, and I will be your teacher. (生物学へようこそ。私はベン・ウィルソン。そしてあなたの先生です) と説明しているため、間違い。
3. は「生徒たちは彼らの授業スケジュールを彼らのシラバスの表で確認できる (見つけることができる)」という意味。最後の段落の序盤に、I want to explain one more thing before you go, so I will talk more quickly. It is about your schedule. It is on the back of your syllabus. (あなたたちが行く前にもう1つ説明したいことがありますので、もっと速く話しますね。〈それは〉あなたたちのスケジュールについてです。〈それは〉あなたたちのシラバスの裏にあります) と話しているため、間違い。
4. は「生徒たちは最初の実験を明日行う予定」という意味。最後の段落の中盤に、We will have the first experiment next week,(私たちは最初の実験を来週行います) と話していることから、実験は翌日に行わないことが分か

る。

1. 生物学へようこそ。私はベン・ウィルソン。そしてあなたたちの先生です。

2. あなたたちは、209教室にいます。

3. （我々には）3人の生物学の先生がいて、みな違う教室で教えていますので、少し紛らわしいかもしれません。

4. あなたたちが正しい場所にいることを望みます。もし違う場合は、手を挙げてください。

5. 1人だけですか？ 先生は誰ですか？ コナー先生？

6. あぁ、彼女の授業は私の授業より難しいですよ。ここに残るべきですね（生徒たちが笑う）。

7. 冗談ですよ。

8. あなたの教室は219なので、廊下に出て、右に曲がり、左手にある4番目の部屋があなたの教室になります。

9. 他のみなさんは？ オーケー。いいですね。みなさんは、正しい場所にいるのだと思います。

10. オーケー。授業初日なので、最初に自己紹介をさせてください。

11. 私はカリフォルニアの小さな町で育ちました。

12. この市よりも小さかったと思いますが、美しくたくさんの自然がありました。

13. 私たちには大きな湖がありました。タッパン湖はこの地域ではけっこう人気があるんですよね？

14. 私たちの湖は、タッパン湖よりも大きくはありませんでしたが、より美しかったと思います。

15. 私の地元にいる一部の人たちはタッパン湖よりも良いと言うかもしれません。

16. 私が小さい男の子だった時は、そこに行き虫を捕まえるのが大好きでした。

17. 私が高校にいた時は、私の好きな科目は生物学でした。

18. 他の科学の授業よりも簡単だと思っていました。

19. 実際、私の生物学の最終成績は化学や物理学の最終成績よりも良かったです。そのため、私

20. 私が大学にいた時、私はたくさんの生物学の授業を取りました。

21. （それらは）高校で受けた（私の）生物学の授業より興味深かったのですが、より難しかったです。

22. 私は本当に熱心に勉強したのですが、私の成績はそこまで良くなかったです。

23. 私は1つも単位（授業）を落とさなかったのですが、いくつかの授業では危なかった（近かった）です。

24. 私は、大学を卒業するのに5年間かかりましたが、私は幸運でした。なぜなら、私はこの仕事を卒業した直後に得たからです。

25. 私には双子の姉（妹）と、弟がいます。姉（妹）は私よりも、はるかに賢いです。

26. 私たちは同じ大学に同じ時に入学しました。

27. 彼女は私よりも熱心に勉強していたとは思わないのですが、彼女は卒業するのに3年半しかかかりませんでした。

28. 彼女も先生として働いていますが、彼女はスペイン語を教えています。

29. 私の弟は、大学にいた時、上手なバスケ選手でした。

30. 彼は私よりはるかに大きいので、一部の人は彼が私の弟だとは信じません。

31. 彼は今何をしているのか？ 彼は、私たちの地元でバスケのコーチとして働いています。

32. オーケー。私については十分ですね。それでは、この授業について話をしましょう。

33. シラバスを配りますので、私のメールアドレス、この授業のゴール、授業のスケジュールなどが分かるでしょう。

34. これについて説明しますが、私はあなたたちを退屈にさせたくないので、10分で終わらせるように挑戦します。

35. 最初に、メールアドレスが右上の角にあるのが見えますか。それが私のメールアドレスです。

36. いつでも私に連絡してください。

37. 次に、この授業の目標（ゴール）について話しましょう……しかし、まず1つあなたたちに

質問をさせてください。

38. もし、答えを知っている場合は、手を挙げてください。いいですか？　生物学とは何でしょう？

39. 何をこの授業で我々は学ぶでしょう？　誰か答えを知っていますか？　誰も知らないのですか？

40. いいでしょう。みんなただ恥ずかしがっているだけだと思います。答えを言いますよ。

41. 生物学とは命についての勉強です。簡単に聞こえますが、そうでもないです。

42. あなたたちに例をあげましょう。これらの2つの写真を見てください。

43. どちらが本物のアヒルでしょう？　もし左側のアヒルが本物だと思う場合は手を挙げて。

44. 私に見えるようにもっと高く手を挙げてください。オーケー。

45. 全ての生徒がこちらを本物のアヒルだと思っているのですね。右のアヒルはどうでしょう？

46. こちらは本物のアヒルだと思いますか？　手を挙げて……高くお願いします。

47. オーケー。誰もいないですね。えっと、あなたたちは正しいです。

48. 左側のは本物のアヒルですが、右側のは違います。しかし、もう1つ質問があります。

49. どうして分かったのですか？　違いは何ですか？　誰か答えられますか？……いいでしょう。

50. 誰も答えられなくて良かったです。なぜなら、もし答えられるようでしたら、この授業を取らないでいいですから。

51. このように、「命」という言葉の意味を理解するのはとても難しいのです。

52. しかし、心配しないで。なぜなら、私たちはこのことについて授業で話しますので。そして、何だと思いますか？

53. 「命」という言葉の意味を理解することは、この授業の主な目標（ゴール）の1つなのです。

54. 難しく聞こえますか？

55. まあ、私はあなたたちに伝えておかないといけないですね。他の科学の授業の方が生物学よりはるかに難しいのですよ。おや、まあ。時間がなくなってきています。オーケー。

56. あなたたちが行く前にもう1つ説明したいことがありますので、もっと速く話しますね。

57. （それは）あなたたちのスケジュールについてです。（それは）あなたたちのシラバスの裏にあります。

58. 私たちは最初の実験を来週行いますので、エプロンを持ってきてください。

59. もし持っていない場合は、スーパーマートに行って1つ買って（手に入れて）ください。（彼らは）安いエプロンを売っています（持っています）から。

60. スーパーマートの（彼らの）エプロンは、（彼らの）ポテトチップスよりも安いと思います。

61. オーケー。今日の分は、これで全てです。また明日会いましょう

7 最上級

解答例

Q1. 2

Q2. 3

Q3. 1

Q4. 財布を落としたら、おそらく一番近くの交番で見つけることができること。

Q5. 4

Q6. 人が多すぎて公園を通ることが困難になるだろうから。

Q7. the Awa Dance Festival (in Tokushima)

Q8. 3

Q9. 1

Q10. 2

解説

Q1. 下線部 (1) の this list（このリスト）の直後に、リストの説明として、It shows the sizes of Asian countries.（これは、アジアの国々の大きさを表しています）と話していることから、リストは「アジアの国々の国土の大きさ」ということが分かる。

Q2. 3段落目で「日本は安全」だということを説明しており、その例として（車ではなく）、Many people in big cities work late and go home by train or bus.（大都市で働く多くの人は遅くまで働き、電車やバスで家に帰ります）と説明している。しかし、下線部 (2) の直後で、Walking outside alone at night is still dangerous in Japan,（夜に1人で歩くことは日本でもやはり危険です）と話していることから、下線部 (2) は「勘違いしないでくださいね」が一番適格だと分かる。

Q3. 下線部 (3) の直後に、Can you believe they have vending machines on the street?（道に自動販売機があるのが信じられますか？）と書かれている。

Q4. 4段落目の終盤で、People are so nice in this country. If you drop your wallet somewhere, you will have a good chance to find it at the closest police box.（この国にいる人たちは、とても優しいです。もしどこかで財布を落としたのなら、一番近くの交番で見つける可能性が高いでしょう）と話している。

Q5. （ア）の直後に party という言葉がきていることから、（ア）に入るのは、パーティーの名前だということが分かる。5段落目の中盤で、Cherry blossoms bloom during this season, and many people enjoy them with their friends, family, students, and so on. They often bring food and drinks and have a party.（この季節には桜が咲き、多くの人たちは友人、家族、教え子などと一緒に桜を〈それらを〉楽しみます。彼らは、たびたび食べ物や飲み物を持ってきてパーティーを開きます）と説明していることから「花見」について話していることが分かる。

Q6. 下線部 (4) は「（それは）最低です」という意味。5段落目で「桜」「花見」についての説明があり、下線部 (4) の前後で、During this season, if you go to a park with beautiful cherry blossoms on weekends, it is the worst. You may not be able to walk through the park because there are too many people.（この季節に、きれいな桜のある公園に週末行こうものなら、最低です。公園を歩いて通ることは、おそらくできないでしょう。なぜなら人が多すぎるからです）と説明している。

Q7. 6段落目の序盤で、ジョンが参加した3つの夏のお祭り（秋田の竿灯まつり、京都の祇園祭、徳島の阿波おどり）についての説明があり、They were great, but I thought the Awa Dance Festival was the best of the three（それらは素晴らしかったのですが、阿波おどりが3つの中で一番だと思いました）と話している。

Q8. 最後から3段落目の序盤で、Leaves change their colors and look beautiful.（葉が色を変え、美しく見えます）と説明している。兵庫の六甲山にあるロープウェイは「そこからの

景色が美しい」という話であって、ロープウェイ自体が美しいわけではないので間違い。

Q9. 最後から2段落目の序盤で、you can see beautiful Christmas lights in winter.（美しいクリスマスのライトを冬には見ることができます）と説明されている。美しいライトで装飾されている場所の例として「大きな公園」や「デパート」が登場しているが「大きな公園でのイベント」や「デパートでの買い物」については触れられていない。

Q10. 2.は、「ジョンは日本の都市部の地域では人々は決して歩かないと思っている」という意味。3段落目で「日本でも夜に1人で歩くのは多少危険」という話はされているが、決して歩かないとは書かれていないので、本文の内容とは異なる。
1.は、「ジョンは日本にいた際、香川に住んでいた」という意味。2段落目の序盤で、I lived in Kagawa Prefecture for three years when I was little.（私は幼い時に香川県に3年間住んでいました）と説明している。
3.は、「ジョンは、冬に御殿場高原リゾートに行くのは良いアイデアだと思っている」という意味。最後から2段落目で日本の冬についての説明があり、One of the most popular places to visit during this season is Gotemba Kogen Resort.（この季節に訪ねる最も人気のある場所の1つは御殿場高原リゾートです）と話している。
4.は、「日本にいる人たちは、春に桜を見ることを楽しむ」という意味。5段落目で日本の春についての説明があり、Cherry blossoms bloom during this season, and many people enjoy them with their friends, family, students, and so on.（この季節には桜が咲き、多くの人たちは友人、家族、教え子などと一緒に桜を〈それらを〉楽しみます）と話している。

全文和訳例

1. おはようございます、みなさん。私は、ジョン・コーリンズ。今日は、日本についてお話

ししします。

2. 多くの人たちは、日本は小さい島国だと思っています。

3. 実際、アメリカより、はるかに小さいです。しかし、6,800より多くの島があります。

4. 実を言うと、世界の中でも小さい国というわけではありません。

5. このリストを見てください。これは、アジアの国々の大きさを表しています。

6. 40より多くの国がリストにあります。

7. 日本が最も小さな国だと思いますか？

8. 答えは「いいえ」です。アジアで最も小さな国はモルディブ共和国です。日本はどうでしょう？

9. 日本は（それは）19位に位置しているので、アジアにある多くの国より実際は大きいのです。

10. 私は幼い時に香川県に3年間住んでいました。香川はどこでしょう？

11. 香川は（それは）四国地方にあり、日本で最も小さい県です。

12. それでは、一番大きいのは？　北海道が全ての中で一番大きいです。

13. 関東地方よりはるかに大きいので、巨大です。

14. 私が日本にいた時、たくさんの興味深いものを見つけましたので、それらについて話させてください。

15. 最初に、日本は安全です。世界で最も安全な国の1つだと思います。

16. 大都市で働く多くの人は遅くまで働き、電車やバスで家に帰ります。

17. アメリカはどうでしょう？　同じことができるとは思えません。

18. もしあなたが都市部で働いていて、いつも遅くまで働く必要があるのなら、あなたの安全のために車で仕事に行くべきでしょう。

19. 勘違いしないでくださいね。

20. 夜に1人で歩くことは日本でもやはり危険です。しかし、暗い中1人で歩きたくないという理由だけで車での通勤を選ぶ人は日本ではごく少数でしょう。

21. そして……これが別の例です。この写真を見てください。

22. （写真を見せる）道に自動販売機があるのが信じられますか？

23. これ（それ）を私たちの国で想像するのは難しいです。なぜなら、道に自動販売機があるのは危険すぎるからです。

24. なぜか？ なぜなら、一部の悪い人たちが（それらから）お金を盗もうとするからです。しかし、日本ではそうではありません。

25. この国にいる人たちは、とても優しいです。

26. もしどこかで財布を落としたのなら、一番近くの交番で見つける可能性が高いでしょう。

27. 他の国々にとっては、普通には聞こえないでしょう。

28. 2番目に、日本は美しいです。なぜ私がそう思うのか？

29. なぜなら、日本のほとんどの地域では4つの季節があり、それぞれの季節で違ったものを楽しむことができるからです。

30. 例えば、春の間は、美しい花を人々は楽しむことができます。

31. この季節には桜が咲き、多くの人たちは友人、家族、教え子などと一緒に桜を（それらを）楽しみます。

32. 彼らは、たびたび食べ物や飲み物を持ってきてパーティーを開きます。

33. この種のパーティーには名前があります。それは、花見パーティーです。

34. この季節に、きれいな桜のある公園に週末行こうものなら、最低です。

35. 公園を歩いて通ることは、おそらくできないでしょう。なぜなら人が多すぎるからです。

36. 夏に日本人は何をするのでしょう？

37. 彼らは花火を見ることや、大きな夏のお祭りに行くことを楽しみます。

38. 多くの人は、それらのイベントに浴衣（夏用の着物）を着ていくので、なかなか興味深いです。私が日本にいた時はいくつかの大きなお祭りに行きました。

39. 例えば、秋田の竿灯まつり、京都の祇園祭、徳島の阿波おどりです。

40. それらは素晴らしかったのですが、阿波おどりが3つの中で一番だと思いました。なぜな

41. ら、踊りに参加することができたからです。

41. とてもワクワクするものでした。踊りはそこまで難しくないので、誰でもできると思います。

42. もし興味があるのなら、インターネットでいくつか動画を見ることができますので、それらを見てみてください。

43. 秋は、日本では色鮮やかな（カラフルな）季節です。葉が色を変え、美しく見えます。

44. 日本にはたくさんの山があります。実際、日本の土地の70%よりも多くの範囲を山がおおっているので、いたる所で美しい木々を楽しむことができます。

45. 私が日本にいた時は、たくさんの山に登りました。そして、（それらは）本当に美しかったです。

46. 私は特に兵庫県の六甲山が好きでした。

47. 全ての中で一番の山だったと思います。

48. ロープウェイがあり、そこからの景色はとても美しいです。

49. もし秋に兵庫を訪ねる機会があれば、六甲山に行くべきです。

50. 最後に、美しいクリスマスのライトを冬には見ることができます。

51. 大きな公園やデパートの多くは、美しいライトで装飾されており、それらのいくつかは無料で見ることができます。

52. この季節に訪ねる最も人気のある場所の1つは御殿場高原リゾートです。

53. 私は数年前に、友人たちとそこに一緒に行きましたが、いくつかの場所は無料で見られたので、素晴らしかったです。

54. ですから、日本は素晴らしい国だと思います。日本では、ハイテクのトイレ、アニメ、寿司なども楽しむことができるので、もし機会があれば日本を訪ねてみてください。

55. 私の発表はこれで終了です。ありがとうございました。

8 原級比較の as 〜 as

（p.126）

解答例

Q1. 梅雨
Q2. 4
Q3. full
Q4. 1
Q5. 4
Q6. 2
Q7. 3
Q8. 1
Q9. （ミツルが作りたいと思っている）英語を無料で学ぶことができるスマートフォン用のゲーム
Q10. 2

解説

Q1. rainy は「雨の / 雨の多い」という意味。rainy season の直訳は「雨の季節 / 雨の多い季節」となる。下線部 (1) の直後にミツルの雨の日の通学について話していることや、少し後に、June is the worst month of the year for me（6月は僕にとって1年の中で最悪の月だよ）と話していることから「梅雨」だということが推測できる。

Q2. 下線部 (2) を含む文は「彼らは、僕と似たような理由でバスを使っているのだと思う」という意味。本文序盤でミツルが通学に関して、I hate the rainy season because I often have to take a bus to go to school. If it is sunny or cloudy, I go to school by bicycle.（僕は梅雨が大嫌いでね。たびたびバスに乗って学校に行かないといけないから。晴れや曇りなら、自転車で行くんだけどね）と説明していることから、ミツルは雨が理由でいつもの交通手段が使えないからバスを使っているのが分かる。

Q3. 下線部 (3) の packed はミツルが乗るバスの説明として使われている。下線部 (3) の少し前で、ミツルがバスで学校に行くことに関して、It's terrible because it is always full.（ひ

どいよ。いつも満員だからね）と説明していることから、packed は満員を表す意味だと分かる。

Q4. 本文中盤で、返却された試験結果に関しての説明がありワカコが、I got 90 on my Math exam and 70 on my Biology exam. My other exam scores were not as good as my Math exam, but they were better than my Biology exam.（数学で90点、生物学で70点取ったよ。他の試験の点数は数学ほど良くはなかったけど、生物学よりは良かったかな）と説明されており、ミツルに関しては I got 75 on my English exam, but that was my highest.（英語で75点を取ったけど、それが僕の最高得点だったよ）と説明している。

Q5. just around the corner は、「角を曲がったところに」「まもなく」という意味の熟語。下線部 (4) が含まれた文は、the summer break is just around the corner（夏休みは just around the corner）なので、下線部 (4) は「夏休みを説明するフレーズ」ということが分かる。下線部 (4) の直後にワカコが、The summer break is going to start in ten days. We will have a lot of homework, but I think we will have enough time to finish it.（夏休みは10日後に始まるね。たくさん宿題があるだろうけど、終わらせるための十分な時間はあると思うな）と発言していることから、宿題はあることが分かる。

Q6. 下線部 (5) の前で、ミツルとワカコは、この夏休みや去年の夏休みについて話しており、ワカコが、Do you have any plans over the break?（the break の間、何か予定はあるの?）とたずねてからミツルが I am planning to take a computer programming course（コンピュータープログラミングのコースを取る予定なんだ）と話していることから、the break は「この夏休み」だと分かる。

Q7. (ア) の直前で、ミツルが夏休みの間に取るコンピュータープログラミングのコースについてワカコが、I want to take that course, too. Do you think it is too late?（私もそのコース

を取りたいな。もう遅すぎると思う?)と締め切りについて質問をし、ミツルがスケジュールを確認した後で、Oh, you are lucky (ア), so you must register as soon as you can. (おや、あなたはラッキーだね。(ア)。だから、できる限り早く登録しないとだめだよ)と書かれているので(ア)に入るのは、3. の、because the deadline is tomorrow(締め切りは明日だから)となる。

1. の意味は「あなたはこのコースを取ることができないから」

2. の意味は「あなたは良いパソコンを持っているから」

4. の意味は「あなたはスマートフォンを持っているから」

Q8. 本文序盤にミツルが、we usually have our final exams in the first week of July(たいてい僕たちは7月の最初の週に期末試験があるから)と発言している。また、本文中盤でワカコが、The summer break is going to start in ten days. (夏休みは10日後に始まるね)と発言している。そして、Q7.からコンピュータープログラミングのコースの締め切りが翌日だとわかる。また、本文終盤でコンピュータープログラミングのコースが始まる時期についてミツルが、It will start in the last week of July. (7月の最後の週に始まる予定だよ)と説明している。(本文に部活についての説明は書かれていないので注意)。

Q9. 下線部(6)が登場するミツルの発言の最初に、I want to make a free game to learn English.(無料で英語を学ぶことができるゲームを作りたいと思っているんだ)と書かれており、なぜミツルが作りたいのかを説明した後に、〜, so I want to make this game.(〜から、僕はこのゲームを作りたいと思っているんだ)と説明している。

Q10. 本文終盤でワカコが、My computer is really old. I think I bought it 7 years ago. Should I get a new one? (私のパソコンは本当に古いんだ。7年前に買ったと思う。新しいのを手に入れるべきかな?)と質問したのに対し、ミツ

ルが、you don't need to get a new computer. (あなたは、新しいパソコンを手に入れる必要はないよ)と答え、ワカコが、Sounds good. (了解)と返答していることから、答えは2. だと分かる。

1. は、本文序盤にミツルが、I like going to school by bicycle. (自転車で学校に行くのは好きなんだ)と発言している。

3. は、本文中盤でミツルが期末試験の結果に関して、My parents were not that happy to see the scores, but 〜. (両親は点数を見てあまり嬉しそうではなかったけど、〜)と発言している。

4. は、本文終盤でミツルが自分が作りたいと思っているスマートフォン用のゲームに関して、I am not really sure if it will be popular (人気が出るかは、はっきりとは分からないかな)と発言している。

全文和訳例

1. ミツル:美しい日だね。梅雨がやっと終わって良かったよ。

2. ワカコ:そうだね。去年ほど雨が降ったとは思わないかな。

3. ミツル:僕は梅雨が大嫌いでね。たびたびバスに乗って学校に行かないといけないから。

4. 晴れや曇りなら、自転車で行くんだけどね。

5. だいたい40分かかるから、少し遠いんだけど、裏道を通れば、大通りより信号が少ないから、けっこう速く行けるんだ。

6. すばらしい景色も楽しむことができるから、自転車で学校に行くのは好きなんだ。

7. だけど、雨が降っていると、僕はバスで学校に行く。なぜなら、そういう時は自転車で学校に行くのが危険になるから。

8. ワカコ:私は、バスで学校に行くのは好きじゃないな。

9. ミツル:僕も好きじゃないかな。ひどいよ。いつも満員だからね。

10. 乗客は主に学生と働いている人たちだから、(彼らは)僕と似たような理由でバスを使っているんだと思う。

29

11. ワカコ：なるほど。

12. ミツル：6月は僕にとって1年の中で最悪の月だよ。学校に行くために満員のバスに約30分間乗るのは、全く楽しくないし、たいてい僕たちは7月の最初の週に期末試験があるから、そのために勉強をしないといけないし。

13. ワカコ：そう。試験。どうだった？

14. ミツル：まぁまぁだったよ。全て試験は戻ってきたの？

15. ワカコ：まだだね。だけど、いくつかは戻ってきたよ。

16. 数学で90点、生物学で70点取ったよ。

17. 他の試験の点数は数学ほど良くはなかったけど、生物学よりは良かったかな。あなたはどうだったの？

18. ミツル：僕のは、そこまで良くなかったよ。あなたほど熱心に勉強しなかったからね。

19. 英語で75点を取ったけど、それが僕の最高得点だったよ。

20. 両親は点数を見てあまり嬉しそうではなかったけど、関係ないかな。

21. 世界の終わりではないし、夏休みは、もうすぐそこだからね。待てないよ。

22. ワカコ：そうだね。夏休みは10日後に始まるね。

23. たくさん宿題があるだろうけど、終わらせるための十分な時間はあると思うな。

24. ミツル：わかるよ。夏は好きだな。僕たちは学校に行かないでいいから。だけど、暑い（気温の高い）日は好きじゃないな。

25. どんどん暑くなってきているよ！

26. もし長時間（長すぎる間）外にいたら、ひょっとすると死んでしまうからね。冗談じゃなく。

27. 僕たちは去年サッカーの試合をキャンセルしなくちゃいけなかったんだ。（なぜなら）外が暑すぎたから。

28. ワカコ：わかる。天気予報によると8月は更にひどくなるみたいだから、去年ほど悪くならないことを願いましょう（望みましょう）。

29. 休みの間、何か予定はあるの？

30. ミツル：コンピュータープログラミングのコースを取る予定なんだ。（なぜなら）スマートフォン用のゲームを作りたいから。（そして）僕たちの高校ではあまり（それについて）習うことができないしね。

31. ワカコ：なるほど。

32. ミツル：屋外での授業は全くないだろうから、熱中症になる心配は、しなくていいからね。

33. ワカコ：ははは。それはそうだね。何だと思う？　興味深そうだね（それは興味深く聞こえるね）。

34. 私もそのコースを取りたいな。もう遅すぎると思う？

35. ミツル：確認させて。僕のスマートフォンにスケジュールが入っていたと思うから……

36. おや、あなたはラッキーだね。締め切りは明日だから。だから、できる限り早く登録しないとだめだよ。

37. ワカコ：本当？　いいね！　家に戻ったらすぐにするよ。

38. そのコースのために私は何か必要なの？

39. ミツル：自分自身のパソコンを持っている必要があるかな。（1台）借りることはできないだろうから。

40. ワカコ：あらら。私のパソコンは本当に古いんだ。

41. 7年前に買ったと思う。新しいのを手に入れるべきかな？

42. ミツル：僕のパソコンもあなたのと同じぐらい古いと思うよ。

43. 少し遅いけど、コードを書くには十分速いから、あなたは新しいパソコンを手に入れる必要はないよ。

44. ワカコ：了解。コースはいつ始まる予定なの？

45. ミツル：7月の最後の週に始まる予定だよ。

46. コースはたったの5日間なんだけど、（僕たちは）毎日6時間勉強する予定だから、たくさん学べると思うよ。

47. 最後の2日間で単純なスマートフォンのゲームを作る予定だから、とてもワクワクしてね。

48. ワカコ：どんなスマートフォンのゲームを作りたいの？

49. ミツル：無料で英語を学ぶことができるゲー

ムを作りたいと思っているんだ。

50. 教科書から英語を学ぶのは退屈だと思う。だから、英語を学ぶ違う方法を作りたいんだ。

51. 英語学校に放課後や週末に行くということもできるけど、値段が高いだろうから（それは）万人向けではないんだよ（みんなのためのものではないんだよ）。

52. 英語を学ぶ平等な機会は、全ての生徒にあるべきだと思うから、僕はこのゲームを作りたいと思っているんだ。

53. ワカコ：おぉ。それは良いね。

54. ミツル：ありがとう。だけど、人気が出るかは、はっきりとは分からないかな。なぜなら、英語を学ぶことは他の科目を学ぶことよりも重要ではなくなると思うから。

55. ワカコ：なんで、そうじゃなくなるの？

56. ミツル：えっと、なぜなら私たちのスマートフォンは、今では翻訳機として使う（動く）ことができるからだよ。本当に便利でね（良くてね）。

57. 何も問題なく、普通の会話をすることができて、どんどん良くなってきているから、近い将来英語を学ぶ必要がなくなるかもしれない。

58. ワカコ：それは興味深いね。

9　比較級・最上級　応用編

(p.146)

解答例

Q1.　4

Q2.　2

Q3.　3

Q4.　Some students didn't like his class

Q5.　1

Q6.　お金の歴史について

Q7.　2

Q8.　いつ：約1,000年前
　　　どこ：中国

Q9.　4

Q10.　3

解説

Q1. 下線部 (1) の直前で、昨年の成績について話しており、エリックが、Which class was the most difficult? (どの授業が一番難しかったの?) とたずねて、ヒロコが、Chemistry. No doubt. It was (1)a nightmare. I think no other class is more difficult than Chemistry. (化学だね。間違いない。nightmareだったよ。化学より難しい科目は他にはないね) と発言していることから一番適格なのは4.の「悪夢」だと分かる。

Q2. (ア) の前で世界史の成績について話しており、ヒロコが、my final grade was not that good (私の最終的な成績はあまり良くなかったよ) と発言した後にエリックが、What did you get? (何を取ったの?) とたずねていることから、(ア) に入るのはヒロコの世界史の成績だということが分かる。
また (ア) の後でエリックが、I took World History two years ago, and my grade was worse. (僕は世界史を2年前に取って、成績はもっと悪かったから)、I got a C. (Cを取った) と答えていることから、正解は2.のI got a B. (Bを取ったんだ) となる。
1.は「Cだったよ」、3.は「新しいカメラを手に入れたんだ」、4は「新しいパソコンを手に

入れたんだ」という意味。

Q3. ヒロコとエリックの会話の終盤で、エリックがエバンズ先生のEconomics の授業について、he always gave us a question like "What is money?" "How should we use our money?" and "Why things are so expensive today?" at the beginning of each class. (彼はいつも各授業の最初に「お金とは何か?」「私たちはどのように我々のお金を使うべきか?」「なぜ物は昨今こんなに高いのか?」といった質問を僕たちに与えるんだ) と説明していることから、Economics は、お金についての学問である経済学だと分かる。

Q4. complain (不満を言う/苦情を言う) という単語の意味を知らない場合は、文脈から単語の意味を推測できるかがポイント。ヒロコとエリックの会話の終盤で、エリックがエバンズ先生の授業に関して、Some students didn't like his class because of his teaching style. (一部の生徒たちは、彼の授業が好きではなかったです。彼の授業スタイルが理由でね) と発言し、ヒロコがWhat do you mean? (どういう意味?) と聞いている。エリックがエバンズ先生の指導方法 (授業の最初に質問をする、生徒たちは答えを紙に書き提出する) について説明した後で、He usually repeated the answers a few times during class, so it was not that difficult, but a few students were complaining. (彼はたいてい授業の間に何回か答えを繰り返すから、そこまで難しくはなかったんだけど、何人かの生徒たちは不満を言っていたね) と発言しているので、下線部 (3) と似た意味の部分は、Some students didn't like his class (一部の生徒たちは彼の授業が好きではなかったです) となる。

Q5. ヒロコとエリックの会話の中盤で、Actually, I have Economics next period. (実は経済学の授業が次にあるんだ) と発言したのに対しエリックが、Oh, do you have to go now? (え、今行かないといけない?) と質問し、ヒロコが、No. I need to go to the library before the class, but ~ (いいや。授業に行く前に図書館

に行く必要があるんだけど、~) と答えていることから、会話の後で向かったのは図書館だと分かる。

Q6. ジョンソン先生が授業の冒頭で、As I announced last time, we are going to talk about the history of money today. (前回の授業で話した通り、今日私たちはお金の歴史について話します) と説明している。

Q7. 下線部 (4) の前後でお金について、Many people work very hard to earn them. Some people try to steal them from other people, and it gets worse sometimes. In other words, money has so much power. (多くの人々は、それら〈硬貨や紙幣〉を得るためにとても熱心に働きます。一部の人たちは他の人々からそれらを盗もうとし、更に悪いことにも時々なります。違う言葉で言えば、お金にはすごい力があるということです) と説明している。下線部 (4) は「お金を盗むことよりも悪い事」なので、答えは2.の「お金のために人生を台無しにするような重い罪を犯すこと」だと分かる。

Q8. ジョンソン先生の授業の4段落目の最初に、How about paper money? Chinese people invented the first paper money about 1,000 years ago, (紙幣はどうでしょう? 約1,000年前に中国の人たちが最初の紙幣を発明しました) と書かれている。問題は「最初のお金」ではなく「最初の紙幣」なのがポイント (「最初のお金」に関しては、3段落目の最初に書かれている)。

Q9. 下線部 (5) の前で、Chinese people invented the first paper money about 1,000 years ago, but many people didn't like the idea first. Why? That'll be the first question on this worksheet. (約1,000年前に中国の人たちが最初の紙幣を発明しました。しかし、多くの人たちは当初この考えが好きではありませんでした。なぜでしょう? それがこのワークシートの最初の質問です) と説明されており直後に、When you get one, I want you to start talking with your neighbors and write down your answer. I will give you 10 minutes.（1枚手に入れましたら、近くの人たちと話し始めて、あなたの答えを書いてください。10分間さしあげます）と説明されていることから、ワークシートは「今から配られるもの」「周りの人たちと一緒に答える」「10分で最初の問題に答えないといけない」ということが分かる（「提出」については本文には書かれていない）。

Q10. 3.は、ヒロコとエリックの会話の終盤でエリックが、Because I took Economics last year and had Prof. Evans.（僕は経済学を去年取って、エバンズ先生だったから）と説明していることから、エバンズ先生は経済学の先生だと分かるので、これが正解。

1.は、ヒロコとエリックの会話の中盤で、ヒロコが自分の化学の成績について、I don't think I got the highest score, but I think I got at least third highest score in my class.（一番高い点数を取ったとは思わないけど、クラスで最低でも3番目に高い点数は取ったと思うよ）と説明している。

2.は、ヒロコとエリックの会話の中盤で、エリックが世界史の授業について、I had to turn in a paper every week, but 〜（毎週レポートを提出しないといけなかったんだけど、〜）と説明している。

4.は、ジョンソン先生の授業の3段落目の最初で、some scientists say people in Turkey made coins about 3,000 years ago, and they were the oldest type of money（一部の科学者は、トルコにいた人たちが約3,000年前に硬貨を作ったと主張しています。そして、それがお金の最も古い形でした）と説明されており、4段落目で、How about paper money? Chinese people invented the first paper money about 1,000 years ago,（紙幣はどうでしょう？　約1,000年前に中国の人たちが最初の紙幣を発明しました）と書かれているため、硬貨、紙幣の順に作られたことが分かる。

1. エリック：やあ、ヒロコ、元気？
2. ヒロコ：眠たいよ。5時に目が覚めて、その後寝られなくなっちゃったから、少し勉強しようと決めたんだ。
3. エリック：わぁ。それは良いことだね。
4. ヒロコ：まぁ、去年、私の成績は良くなかったから、今年はもっと熱心に勉強する必要があってね。
5. エリック：本当？　どの授業が一番難しかったの？
6. ヒロコ：化学だね。間違いない。悪夢だったよ。
7. 化学より難しい科目は他にはないね。
8. 私のクラスにいる他のどの生徒よりも勉強したのは、けっこう確かだと思うけど、私はBを取ったからね。
9. Aを取ろうとしたんだけど、できなかったよ。
10. エリック：まぁ、悪くないじゃん。去年、僕は化学を取ってCを取ったよ。
11. 良い成績ではないのは知っているけど、単位を取る（授業に合格する）ことができたから、嬉しかったね。
12. あなたが、一番高い点数を取ったと思う？
13. ヒロコ：違うと思うな。一番高い点数を取ったとは思わないけど、クラスで最低でも3番目に高い点数は取ったと思うよ。
14. エリック：それは良いね。あなたは自分のことを誇りに思うべきだよ。
15. どの授業が2番目に難しかった？
16. ヒロコ：そうだね。世界史は、けっこう難しかったよ。
17. 人や場所の名前を覚えるのが得意ではないから、私の最終的な成績はあまり良くなかったよ。
18. エリック：何を取ったの？
19. ヒロコ：Bを取ったんだ。
20. エリック：それは良いよ。僕は世界史を2年前に取って、成績はもっと悪かったから。
21. ヒロコ：何を取ったの？
22. エリック：Cを取ったんだ。毎週レポートを提出しないといけなかったんだけど、パソコ

ンを持っていなかったから、図書館でしなくちゃいけなくて。難しかったよ。

23. ヒロコ：本当？　私たちは、授業（コース）を通して、3つのレポートしか書かないでよかったよ。だから、そこまで悪くなかったかな。

24. エリック：今年は何か社会科の科目を取っているの？

25. ヒロコ：うん。2つ取っているよ。経済学とアジアの歴史。

26. エリック：本当に？　それらはどう？　どっちの方がより興味深い？

27. ヒロコ：（それらは）良いよ。経済学の方が興味深いと思う。

28. 実は経済学の授業が次にあるんだ。

29. エリック：え、今行かないといけない？

30. ヒロコ：いいや。授業に行く前に図書館に行く必要があるんだけど、まだ40分あるから、私は大丈夫だよ。

31. エリック：経済学の先生は誰なの？（誰を経済学に持っているの？）

32. ヒロコ：ジョンソン先生だよ（ジョンソン先生を持っているよ）。何で？

33. エリック：（なぜなら）僕は経済学を去年取って、エバンズ先生だったから。

34. 一部の生徒たちは、彼の授業が好きではなかったです。彼の授業スタイルが理由でね。

35. ヒロコ：どういう意味？

36. エリック：えっと、彼はいつも各授業の最初に「お金とは何か？」「私たちはどのように我々のお金を使うべきか？」「なぜ物は昨今こんなに高いのか？」といった質問を僕たちに与えるんだ。

37. 僕たちは、その答えを1枚の紙に書いて授業の最後に彼に渡さないといけなかったんだよ。

38. 彼はたいてい授業の間に何回か答えを繰り返すから、そこまで難しくはなかったんだけど、何人かの生徒たちは不満を言っていたね。

39. ヒロコ：なるほど。ジョンソン先生も時々同じことをすると思うけど、いつもじゃないかな。世界史と経済学は、どちらの方が簡単だった？

40. エリック：経済学。僕は好きだったね。（なぜ

なら）あの授業からたくさんのことを習ったから。

41. ヒロコ：なるほど。あぁ、ごめん。行かなくちゃ。

42. エリック：わかった。またね。
（ジョンソン先生の経済学の授業にて）

43. こんにちは、みなさん。

44. 前回の授業で話した通り、今日私たちはお金の歴史について話します。

45. あなたたちのほとんどが今現在、（あなたたちの）ポケットあるいはカバンの中に何かしらのお金が入っていると思います。

46. 私たちは、硬貨や紙幣を使いますが、私は興味深いと思います。なぜなら、それらはただの金属のかけらと紙だからです。

47. 考えてみて。なぜ私たちは、それらがそんなにも価値があると信じているのでしょう？

48. 多くの人々は、それら（硬貨や紙幣）を得るためにとても熱心に働きます。

49. 一部の人たちは他の人々からそれらを盗もうとし、更に悪いことにも時々なります。

50. 違う言葉で言えば、お金にはすごい力があるということです。

51. 多くの人たちは、できる限りたくさんのお金を手に入れようとします。しかし、なぜでしょう？

52. いつの時代も（いつも）このようだったのでしょうか？　最初のお金はどこから来たのでしょう？

53. いつ人々はそれ（お金）を作ったのでしょう？なぜ人々は作ったのでしょう？

54. 硬貨と紙幣のどちらの種類のお金を人々は先に作ったのでしょう？

55. 私たちはこれらの種類の質問に答えていきます。それでは、始めていきましょう。

56. もしかするとあなたたちも知っているかもしれませんが、人々は硬貨や紙幣を発明する前は、たくさんの違う物をお金として使っていました。

57. 例えば、ある地域の人たちは牝牛や羊をお金として使っていました。

58. ある他の地域の人たちは貝を使っていました。

そのため、人々は何かしらのお金は持っていたのですが、それらは同じ（物）ではありませんでした。

59. それでは、最初のお金はどこから来たのでしょう？

60. 答えは……分かりません。しかし、一部の科学者は、トルコにいた人たちが約3,000年前に硬貨を作ったと主張しています。そして、それがお金の最も古い形でした。

61. なぜ彼らは硬貨を作ったのでしょう？　なぜなら、彼らは税金を政府に払わないといけなかったからです。

62. それが主な理由でした。しかし、彼らはすぐに物を買うことや売ることのためにも硬貨を使い始めました。なぜなら、硬貨は持ち運びが、はるかに簡単だったからです。

63. 紙幣はどうでしょう？

64. 約1,000年前に中国の人たちが最初の紙幣を発明しました。しかし、多くの人たちは当初この考えが好きではありませんでした。

65. なぜでしょう？　それがこのワークシートの最初の質問です。

66. 1枚手に入れましたら、近くの人たちと話し始めて、あなたの答えを書いてください。

67. 10分間さしあげます。もし質問がある場合は、私に教えてください。議論（ディスカッション）の後で、あなたたちの考えをクラスに発表して（共有して）もらいたいので、準備しておいて。分かりましたか？　それでは、始めましょう。

10　原級比較 応用編 & 文頭で使われる接続詞

（p.162）

解答例

Q1.　1

Q2.　3

Q3.　1. タンパク質が豊富だから。
　　　2. 魚や肉を手に入れるのが難しかったから。

Q4.　the population of the world is increasing / the world population will reach around 10 billion in 2050

Q5.　（以下の4つのうちの2つが書かれていれば正解）
　　　・たくさんの水が必要
　　　・たくさんの食べ物が必要
　　　・たくさんの土地が必要
　　　・（昆虫を育てるよりも）時間がかかる

Q6.　多くの人にとって昆虫を食べるという考え（アイデア）は受け入れがたいものだから

Q7.　一番人気のないメニューになる

Q8.　試しに食べてみること

Q9.　4

Q10. 2

解説

Q1.　下線部（1）が含まれる文で、Some scientists say no other food is as <u>nutritious</u> as insects because they have a lot of protein, minerals, and vitamins.（一部の科学者たちは、昆虫ほどnutritiousなものはないと言っています。なぜなら、〈それらには〉豊富なタンパク質、ミネラル、ビタミンが含まれているからです）と書かれていることから、nutritious は「栄養がある」という意味だと分かる。

Q2.　1段落目の終盤で、at least two billion people in the world eat insects as daily food. The world population is now 7.5 billion, so ～.（最低でも世界にいる20億人もの人が昆虫を日常食品として食べています。世界の人口は現在75億人なので、～）と書かれているの

で、20 ÷ 75 = 0.2666…なので、約27%となる。

Q3. 2段落目の中盤で、eating *inago* was pretty common for people in Nagano Prefecture. Why? Because *inago* have high protein, and buying fish and meat was difficult for people in the mountain areas. (長野県の人たちにとってイナゴを食べることは、かなり一般的でした。なぜでしょう？　なぜなら、イナゴはタンパク質が豊富で、魚や肉を買うことは山岳地域に住む人たちには困難だったからです) と書かれている。

Q4. まず food shortage の意味が、下線部 (2) の直後で、What does that mean? It means we will not have enough food for everyone. (それはどういう意味でしょう？　それは、十分な量の食べ物が全員にはないだろうという意味です) と書かれているため「food shortage = 食糧不足」だと分かる。そして食糧不足の理由が、下線部 (2) を含む文で、the world population will reach around 10 billion in 2050, and we will face a problem of food shortage. (世界の人口は2050年には100億人に達します。そのため〈そして〉我々は食糧不足の問題に直面するでしょう) と書かれている。また、1つ前の文で、This is important because the population of the world is increasing. (これは重要です。なぜなら、世界の人口が増加しているからです) とも書かれているので、こちらでも可。

Q5. 3段落目の中盤で、Should we produce more beef? I don't think so. (我々は、もっと牛肉を生産するべきでしょうか？　私はそうとは思いません) と答えた後に、Because cows eat a lot of food and drink a lot of water, raising cows is expensive. (牛はたくさんの食べ物を食べ、たくさんの水を飲むため、育てるのは高額なのです) と理由が書かれている。またその後に It also needs a large area because cows are big, (広い土地も必要です。なぜなら、牛は大きいからです) と書かれている。

また、3段落の序盤に、Because insects grow faster than cows, (昆虫は牛よりも早く成長する) と書かれているので、牛を育てるのは昆虫を育てるより時間がかかることが分かる。

Q6. 下線部 (3) は「ことはそんなに簡単ではありません」という意味。下線部 (3) の直後で、As you know, accepting the idea of eating insects is difficult for many people. (お分かりの通り、多くの人にとって昆虫を食べるという考えは受け入れがたいものです) と書かれている。

Q7. 4段落目の中盤で、If a hamburger restaurant in America sells insect burgers, they will be the least popular food on the menu. (もしアメリカにあるハンバーガーレストランで昆虫バーガーが売られたら、メニューの中で一番人気のない食べ物になるでしょう) と説明されている。

Q8. 5段落目の序盤で「変なものを食べるのは別に目新しいことではない」ということが書かれており、段落の中盤で、We just need to try eating them. (我々は、とりあえず試しに食べてみる必要があります) と書かれている。

Q9. 最後の段落で、著者は「いくらか昆虫を食べることができるため、メキシコに行く」ということが書かれており、下線部 (4) の直前で、It will be my first time eating insects. I hope I will be able to eat some. (昆虫を食べるのは私にとって初めての機会になるでしょう。いくらか食べられることを願っています) と書かれてあるため、答えは「幸運を祈ってください」となる。

Q10. 1.は、2段落目の終盤で、After World War II, people started using strong pesticides to kill *inago*, so the number of *inago* decreased. (第二次世界大戦後は、イナゴを殺すために強い殺虫剤を使い始めたので、イナゴの数は減少しました) と書かれている。

3.は、3段落目の中盤で、producing 1 kg of beef needs about 10 kg of food and 20,000 L of water. (1キロの牛肉を生産するのに約10キロの食べ物と2万リットルの水が必要とさ

れています）と書かれている。

4. は、5段落目の終盤に、Although we cannot imagine yet that we may start seeing insects on our plates more often, I am sure that day will come in the near future.（お皿に昆虫が乗っているのをもっと頻繁に見かけるようになるということを想像するのは、まだ我々にはできませんが、近い将来その日が来ることを確信しています）と書かれている。

全文和訳例

1. 昆虫が世界を救う

2. もしあなたが、安くて健康的な食べ物を探しているのであれば、昆虫を試してみるべきです。

3. あなたは「何を考えているの？　頭がおかしいの？」と思うかもしれません。しかし、昆虫（それら）は、全く悪いものではありません。

4. 一部の科学者たちは、昆虫ほど栄養があるものはないと言っています。なぜなら、（それらには）豊富なタンパク質、ミネラル、ビタミンが含まれているからです。

5. 昆虫は、更に牛肉よりも脂肪分が少ないため牛肉を食べるかわりに昆虫を食べる方がいい考えかもしれません。

6. （ハンバーガーにはたくさんの脂肪が含まれているため、あまりたくさん食べるべきではありません。しかし、昆虫バーガーならあなたが好きなだけ食べることができるかもしれません）。

7. 一部の人たちは、それは変で、少数の人しか昆虫を好んで食べないと思うかもしれませんが、それは本当ではありません。

8. 実際、国際連合食糧農業機関（FAO）によると、最低でも世界にいる20億人もの人が昆虫を日常食品として食べています。

9. 世界の人口は現在75億人なので、その数はそこまで低くないのです。

10. 昆虫を食べることは、貧しい国々だけで起きていることではありません。

11. 日本のようなハイテクな国でも起きています。

12. 例を出しましょう。日本にいる人たちはイナゴ（バッタ）を食べます。

13. 第二次世界大戦の前は、山岳地域にいた人たちはイナゴをよく食べていました。

14. 例えば、長野県の人たちにとってイナゴを食べることは、かなり一般的でした。

15. なぜでしょう？　なぜなら、イナゴはタンパク質が豊富で、魚や肉を買うことは山岳地域に住む人たちには困難だったからです。

16. 第二次世界大戦後は、イナゴを殺すために強い殺虫剤を使い始めたので、イナゴの数は減少しました。

17. 今日、日本の大都市でイナゴを探すのは難しくなってきていますが、一部のスーパーでは、まだ見つけることができます。

18. どのように食べるのでしょう？

19. ご飯と一緒に食べるのは、けっこう一般的です。そのため、まさに牛肉を食べるように（それらを）食べることができます。

20. それだけではありません。昆虫は牛よりも早く成長するので、昆虫を生産する方が牛肉を生産するより、はるかに簡単なのです。

21. なぜこれが重要なのでしょう？

22. これは重要です。なぜなら、世界の人口が増加しているからです。

23. 国際連合によると、世界の人口は2050年には100億人に達します。そのため（そして）我々は食糧不足の問題に直面するでしょう。

24. それはどういう意味でしょう？　それは、十分な量の食べ物が全員にはないだろうという意味です。

25. 違う言葉で言えば、私たちはもっと食べ物を生産する方法を見つける必要があるだろうということです。

26. 多くの科学者たちは、地球温暖化が原因で農業のための土地は将来減るだろうと考えています。

27. 高い気温は、野菜や植物を育てる際の問題も引き起こすので、私たちは何をするべきでしょう？

28. 我々は、もっと牛肉を生産するべきでしょうか？　私はそうとは思いません。

29. なぜなら牛はたくさんの食べ物を食べ、たくさんの水を飲むため、育てるのは高額なのです。

30. 一部の研究によると、1キロの牛肉を生産するのに約10キロの食べ物と2万リットルの水が必要とされています。

31. 広い土地も必要です。なぜなら、牛は大きいからです。そのため、もし我々が牛肉を生産し続けるようなら、我々は食べ物と土地を更に失うことになるでしょう。

32. 昆虫を育てるのはどうでしょう？

33. 牛を育てるほどお金も土地も必要ない（かからない）ので、昆虫を食べることは、この問題を解決する1つの方法になるでしょう。

34. また、もっと食べ物を生産するための新しい技術を開発するより、はるかに簡単でしょう。

35. FAOは、昆虫が将来我々の主食になるかもしれないと言っています。

36. 多くの企業がこのビジネスに興味を持っており、一部の研究者は、その市場は次の10年で大幅に成長すると考えています。

37. もし日本に住んでいるのであれば、今日見ている倍の数のイナゴを見ることになるかもしれません。

38. そのため、私たちは食糧不足の問題を、昆虫を食べることで解決できそうなのですが、ことはそんなに簡単ではありません。

39. お分かりの通り、多くの人にとって昆虫を食べるという考えは受け入れがたいものです。

40. 昆虫は安くて栄養があることを理解していても、お皿の上に昆虫が乗っているのを見たいと思う人はあまり多くないでしょう。なぜなら、彼らにとって昆虫はまだ食べ物ではないのですから。

41. もしアメリカにあるハンバーガーレストランで昆虫バーガーが売られたら、メニューの中で一番人気のない食べ物になるでしょう。

42. もしあなたが、（あなたの住まいに）友だちを夕食に招き昆虫を出したら、彼らはあなたがふざけていると思うでしょう。

43. 彼らが怒り、あなたの住まいに二度と来ないと決めたとしても、私は驚かないでしょう。

44. そうすると、それは我々にとって昆虫を食べるのは不可能だろうということを意味するでしょうか？

45. 答えは「いいえ」です。なぜなら、変なものを食べるのは別に目新しいことではないからです。

46. 考えてみてください。アジアに住む人たちは、カエル、犬、蛇、馬を食べます。

47. フランスにいる人たちは、カタツムリを食べますので、我々はすでに変なものを食べているのです。

48. 我々は、とりあえず試しに食べてみる必要があります。（それらは）美味しいかもしれません。誰が分かるのでしょう？

49. お皿に昆虫が乗っているのをもっと頻繁に見かけるようになるということを想像するのは、まだ我々にはできませんが、近い将来その日が来ることを確信しています。

50. この数年で起きるかもしれません。

51. 私は、来月メキシコを訪ねる計画を立てています。

52. なぜでしょう？　なぜなら、（そこでは）いくらか昆虫を食べられると聞いたからです。

53. 昆虫を食べるのは私にとって初めての機会になるでしょう。いくらか食べられることを願っています。幸運を祈ってください。

最終回　まとめのテスト

(p.178)

解答例

Q1. 1. よく寝ること
　　2. 朝食を食べること
Q2. 2
Q3. 3
Q4. 学校の始まる時間を遅くすること
Q5. 1. ○　2. ○　3. ×　4. ×
Q6. 4
Q7. 1. お腹がすいていない
　　2. 朝食をとるための十分な時間がない
Q8. 1
Q9. （子どもたちの）親
Q10. 2

解説

Q1. 最初の段落の終盤で、because you can improve your grades by sleeping well and eating breakfast,（あなたは、よく寝ることと朝食を食べることで成績を上げることができるからです）と書かれている。

Q2. 下線部（1）の含まれる文は、If you get enough sleep, you will not feel sleepy or tired, so you will be able to concentrate on studying.（十分な睡眠を得ていれば、眠たい、疲れているとは感じないでしょうから、勉強にconcentrate できるでしょう）という意味なので、一番適格なのは2.の「集中する」だと分かる。

Q3. 3段落目に高校生が十分睡眠を取るのが難しい理由が書かれている。段落の序盤に、It is not because they are lazy.（それは、彼らが怠慢だからというわけではありません）と書かれているため、3.が答え。
1.については、If they are playing sports or working part-time, they will have to do their homework after they finish those.（もし彼らがスポーツやアルバイトをしていたら、宿題はそれらが終わった後でしないといけなくなるでしょう）と書かれている。

2.については、Social Networking Services (SNS) can also cause some problems（ソーシャルネットワーキングサービス〈SNS〉もいくらか問題を引き起こす可能性があります）と書かれている。
4.については、they usually get much more homework than elementary or junior high school students do.（彼らには、小学校や中学校の時より、はるかに多くの宿題がたいてい課されます）と書かれている。

Q4. 4段落目の中盤に、Because many high school students in America have to be at school before 8:00 a.m., some researchers are trying to change it to 8:30 a.m. or later.（アメリカにいる多くの高校生は午前8：00前には、学校にいないといけないため、一部の研究者は午前8：30かそれ以降に変えようとしています）と書かれている。また、次の文章で、Some researchers in England say high schools should start at 10:00 a.m. because students are too tired.（イングランドの一部の研究者は午前10：00以降に高校を始めるべきだと言っています）と書かれている。

Q5. 5段落目に朝食がもたらす効果について書かれている。
1.は、Eating breakfast will also change your mood,（朝食を食べることは、あなたの気分も変えてくれます）と書かれているため○。
2.は、Many scientists believe breakfast is the most important meal of the day because it gives you energy and tells your body to wake up.（多くの科学者たちは、朝食が1日で一番重要な食事だと信じています。なぜなら、エネルギーを与え、体を起こしてくれるからです）と書かれているため○。
3.と4.については書かれていないので×。

Q6. 下線部（2）を含む文では、Eating breakfast will also change your mood, and some data show that skipping breakfast will make you fat because you will eat more at night, so if you want to have a great school life, eating a good breakfast is very important.（朝食を

食べることは、あなたの気分も変えてくれます。また、一部のデータはskipping breakfastが肥満に繋がることを表しています。なぜなら、夜にもっと食べてしまうからです。それなので、素晴らしい学校生活を送りたいのであれば、良い朝食を食べることはとても重要なのです）と「朝食をとる重要性」が説明されていることから、正解は4.となる。

Q7. 6段落目の中盤で日本人の小・中学生が朝食を食べない理由として、Many students say they are not hungry or do not have enough time to eat breakfast in the morning.（多くの生徒たちはお腹がすいていない、朝食を食べる十分な時間が朝にないと言っています）と書かれている。

Q8. 最後から3段落目の中盤で朝食について、You should eat vegetables and fruit because they have a lot of vitamins and minerals.（野菜とフルーツを食べるべきです。なぜなら、たくさんのビタミンとミネラルが含まれているからです）、Eating eggs and yogurt is also good because you can get protein.（卵とヨーグルトを食べるのも良いです。なぜなら、タンパク質を得られるからです）、You also need carbohydrates, so don't forget to eat rice or bread.（炭水化物も必要なので、お米やパンを食べることも忘れずに）と書かれているため、これら全てが含まれている1.が正解となる。

Q9. 最後から2段落目の序盤に、providing a nutritious breakfast is very important for students' learning, so, who is going to prepare it? My answer is "parents."（栄養のある朝食を生徒たちに提供するのは生徒たちの学習には重要なのですが、誰が準備するのでしょう？　私の答えは「親」です）と書かれている。

Q10. 2.は、5段落目の序盤に、Many scientists believe breakfast is the most important meal of the day because it gives you energy and tells your body to wake up.（多くの科学者たちは、朝食が1日で一番重要な食事だと

信じています。なぜなら、エネルギーを与え、体を起こしてくれるからです）と書かれているため「夕食の次に朝食は重要」というのは本文の内容と異なる。

1.は、2段落目の終盤に、Some students study all night before their tests, but that is not a good idea.（一部の生徒たちは、テストの前日に一晩中勉強しますが、それは良い考えではありません）と書かれている。

3.は、2段落目の序盤に、Older people usually sleep less, so it is OK if your parents sleep less than eight hours.（年配の人たちの方がたいてい睡眠は短いので、あなたの両親の睡眠時間が8時間より短かったとしても大丈夫です）と書かれている。

4.は、6段落目の中盤に、According to MEXT, about 5% of 6th graders and about 8% of 3rd year junior high school students do not eat breakfast.（文部科学省によると、小学6年生の約5%、中学3年生の約8%が朝食を食べていないとか）と書かれている。

全文和訳例

1. もし良い成績を取りたいならよく寝て朝食を食べよう！

2. あなたが学生なら、成績を良くしたいと思いますか？

3. もし「はい」と答えたなら、あと2つ質問させてください。

4. 毎日何時間寝ますか？　毎朝朝食を食べますか？

5. あなたは「なぜこれらの質問をするの？　なぜそれらが関係あるの？」と思うかもしれないので、理由を言いましょう。

6. 私がそれらの質問をしたのは、あなたは、よく寝ることと朝食を食べることで成績を上げることができるからです。しかし、勘違いしないで。

7. 良い成績を取るために熱心に勉強しないでもいいとは言っていません。

8. 私が言っているのは、よく寝ることと朝食を食べることは熱心に勉強するのと同じぐらい

40

重要だということです。

9. 〈寝ること〉それでは、何時間私たちは寝るべきなのでしょう？

10. 多くの科学者は毎日8時間ぐらい学生たち（生徒たち）は寝るべきだという点に関して同意しています。

11. （年配の人たちの方がたいてい睡眠は短いので、あなたの両親の睡眠時間が8時間より短かったとしても大丈夫です）

12. 十分な睡眠を得ていれば、眠たい、疲れているとは感じないでしょうから、勉強に集中できるでしょう。

13. それだけではありません。一部の研究では、しっかり寝ると、間違いの数も減るということが示されています。

14. それはどういう意味でしょう？ それは、寝ないで勉強することは悪いという意味です。

15. 一部の生徒たちは、テストの前日に一晩中勉強しますが、それは良い考えではありません。

16. もしテストで良い点数を取りたいのであれば、前日に全てをカバーしようとするべきではないです。

17. しかし、多くの高校生にとって毎日約8時間寝るのは難しいです。

18. それは、彼らが怠慢だからというわけではありません。

19. それは、彼らが（彼らの）生活の中でたくさんの変化に直面しているからです。

20. 例えば、彼らには、小学校や中学校の時より、はるかに多くの宿題がたいてい課されます。

21. もし彼らがスポーツやアルバイトをしていたら、宿題はそれらが終わった後でしないといけなくなるでしょう。

22. 更に、ソーシャルネットワーキングサービス（SNS）もいくらか問題を引き起こす可能性があります。そのため、一部の生徒たちは常に疲れており、十分な睡眠を得るのは、彼らにとっては困難となるのです。

23. 寝ることは、身体を強く健康にもします。

24. ある調査研究では、よく寝ないと体重が増えるかもしれないということを示しています。そのため、睡眠を十分とるというのはとても重

25. しかし、多くの生徒にとってそれは困難です。そのため、私たちは何かする必要があります。

26. これを改善する一つの方法は、学校のスケジュールを変えることです。

27. 難しく聞こえますが、アメリカとイングランドの一部の研究者はこれを実現しようとしています。

28. アメリカにいる多くの高校生は午前8:00前には、学校にいないといけないため、一部の研究者は午前8:30かそれ以降に変えようとしています。

29. イングランドの一部の研究者は午前10:00以降に高校を始めるべきだと言っています。なぜなら、生徒たちが疲れすぎているからです。

30. 彼らは、これらの変化は生徒の学校生活をより意味のあるものにすると考えています。

31. 〈朝食を食べること〉それでは、朝食について話しましょう。あなたは毎朝朝食を食べますか？

32. 朝食を食べることは、よく寝ることと同じぐらい重要です。

33. 多くの科学者たちは、朝食が1日で一番重要な食事だと信じています。なぜなら、エネルギーを与え、体を起こしてくれるからです。

34. もしあなたが学生なら、朝食を食べてあなたの1日を始めるというのは素晴らしい方法です。なぜなら、朝の授業を乗り切るための十分なエネルギーを与えてくれるからです。

35. 実際、多くの科学者たちは、朝食を食べることと学生の成績には強い関係があると同意しています。

36. 言い換えれば、もし良い成績を取りたいのであれば、朝食を食べるべきだということです。

37. 朝食を食べることは、あなたの気分も変えてくれます。また、一部のデータは朝食を抜くことが肥満に繋がることを表しています。なぜなら、夜にもっと食べてしまうからです。それなので、素晴らしい学校生活を送りたいのであれば、良い朝食を食べることはとても重要なのです。

38. しかし、日本の子どもたちの一部は学校に行

く前に朝食を食べず、それが深刻な問題になっています。

39. 文部科学省によると、小学6年生の約5%、中学3年生の約8%が朝食を食べていないとか。

40. 理由は何でしょう？

41. 多くの生徒たちはお腹がすいていない、朝食を食べる十分な時間が朝にないと言っています。

42. 数字はまだ低いですが、増加しているため、止める方法を見つけなくてはいけません。

43. 私が言った通り、朝食を食べることはとても重要です。しかし、朝食に何を食べてもかまわないという意味ではありません。

44. 栄養のある食べ物を食べるのがベストですので、朝食にお菓子は食べるべきではありません。

45. 野菜とフルーツを食べるべきです。なぜなら、たくさんのビタミンとミネラルが含まれているからです。

46. 卵とヨーグルトを食べるのも良いです。なぜなら、タンパク質を得られるからです。

47. 炭水化物も必要なので、お米やパンを食べることも忘れずに。

48. この種類の朝食を準備するのは難しいということ知っています。しかし、栄養のある朝食を生徒たちに提供するのは生徒たちの学習には重要なのですが、誰が準備するのでしょう？

49. 私の答えは「親」です。

50. もし、親が自分の子どもたちによく学び、良い成績を取ってもらいたいのであれば、（彼らは）良い朝食を提供することで子どもたちを支援しないといけません。なぜなら、たいてい朝に子どもたちは（朝食を）作るための時間がないからです。

51. 親が子どもたちのために授業に行きテストを受けることができないので、良い朝食を作ることは（彼らの）子どもたちを支援する重要な方法なのです。

52. 自分の子どもたちの成績が悪い場合、多くの親は子どもたちに熱心に勉強しなさいと言います。しかし、子どもたちが（彼らが）十分な睡眠を得ていない、良い朝食を食べていないという場合は、熱心に勉強しなさいと彼らに言うだけでは問題が解決されないかもしれません。

53. もしあなたが親で、子どもの成績に対して快く思っていないのであれば、私はあなたに2つ質問をしたいです。あなたの子どもは十分な睡眠を取っていますか？ そして、彼・彼女に良い朝食を作っていますか？